Hands-on Culture of Mexico and Central America

Kate O'Halloran

Dedication

Por mi madre y mi hija.

User's Guide to Walch Reproducible Books

As part of our general effort to provide educational materials which are as practical and economical as possible, we have designated this publication a "reproducible book." The designation means that purchase of the book includes purchase of the right to limited reproduction of all pages on which this symbol appears:

Here is the basic Walch policy: We grant to individual purchasers of this book the right to make sufficient copies of reproducible pages for use by all students of a single teacher. This permission is limited to a single teacher, and does not apply to entire schools or school systems, so institutions purchasing the book should pass the permission on to a single teacher. Copying of the book or its parts for resale is prohibited.

Any questions regarding this policy or requests to purchase further reproduction rights should be addressed to:

Permissions Editor
J. Weston Walch, Publisher
321 Valley Street • P. O. Box 658
Portland, Maine 04104-0658

1 2 3 4 5 6 7 8 9 10

ISBN 0-8251-3743-8

Printed in the United States of America

Contents

Subject Area Correlation

	Social Studies	English/Language Arts	Foreign Language	Art	Music	Math
Clues to the Region	x					
Economy and Trade in Mexico and Central America	x			x		x
There's a Proverb That Says . . .	x	x				
Central American Folktales	x	x				
The Maya Codex	x			x		x
A Conversation in . . .	x	x	x			
Mexican Tin Ornaments	x			x		
Cooking of Mexico	x					
Panama: Molas	x			x		
Appellidos: Getting the Name Right	x	x				
Music in Central America	x			x	x	
Nearika: Yarn Paintings	x			x		
Tree of Life	x			x		
Day of the Dead	x			x		
Wooden Toys	x			x		
The Mexican Mural Tradition	x			x		
Shopping in Mexico: The Tiangui	x			x		x
Connect-the-Dots Geography	x			x		x

How to Use This Book

This book, like the others in the *Hands-on Culture* series by J. Weston Walch, Publisher, has been designed to help middle school teachers integrate the study of a culture into the curriculum. Textbooks can teach students about the history and geography of an area, but to gain any real understanding, students must also be exposed to the art and traditions of a culture. *Hands-on Culture of Mexico and Central America* provides 18 ready-to-use activities to help you do just that. Through the projects in this book, students will be exposed to the economy, music, literature, and visual arts of Mexico and Central America.

Most of the projects in this book work well either as individual projects or as group activities. You should read both the teacher notes and student pages completely before presenting the activity to students. When a project requires setting up a work station, as in the tree of life and cooking projects, you may find it best to divide the class into groups and set up several work areas. You may also find a group approach helpful for some of the other projects. As students deal with such unfamiliar material as the Maya language, they may find it less intimidating to work together to find solutions.

By their nature, all these projects are interdisciplinary. All are appropriate for a social studies class. Most are appropriate for an art class. Some activities are also appropriate for other subject areas; the correlation chart on the facing page presents these links. Some activities could be done in several different classes.

All the projects have been structured so that the teacher presenting the activity does not need to know either the historical context for an activity or the procedure for doing the project. Full background details are provided where needed. You can share some or all of this information with students if you wish, but it is not necessary for student completion of the project. The step-by-step student instructions for the activities should need no other explanation. All activities have been tested with middle school and high school students.

To help demonstrate the process, you may find it helpful to keep one or two examples of student work for each activity. The next time you present the activity, show the student work as models. When dealing with unfamiliar material, students often find it helpful to have a general idea of what is expected of them. I hope that you and your students enjoy this book and that it helps deepen your students' understanding and appreciation of the cultures of Mexico and Central America.

Clues to the Region

Teacher Guide Page

Objectives

Social Studies

- Students will be familiar with characteristics of the nations of Central America.
- Students will recognize countries by their descriptions.

Materials

Clues to the Region handout

Background

When students study a region, there is often a tendency to lump all the countries in the region together, rather than to see them as separate nations with their own distinct characteristics. In this activity, students will use clues to identify the eight countries that make up Central America and Mexico.

Procedure

1. Distribute the handout. As a class, brainstorm what students know about the region as a whole and about the separate countries in the region.
2. Students proceed as directed on the handout.

Answers

Belize: 9. 14. 18. 28.

Costa Rica: 3. 22.

El Salvador: 6. 19. 32.

Guatemala: 1. 4. 16. 24. 27.

Honduras: 10. 21. 29. 33.

Mexico: 5. 7. 11. 15. 20. 23. 31.

Nicaragua: 12. 17. 26. 30.

Panama: 2. 8. 13. 25.

Variation

The activity can be done as a matching exercise for individual students or as a game for small groups—or even for the class as a whole. To conduct the activity as a group game, divide the class into teams. You can give each team clues for one country and have them figure out which country it is, give all groups clues for all countries and have groups match all clues with countries, or present the game as a tournament where you read one clue to each team in turn and the team must identify the country.

Name ______________________________ Date ______________

Clues to the Region

The eight countries of Mexico and Central America connect North America and South America. They have many things in common; that's why it makes sense to look at them together, as a region. But they have many differences also. How well do you know the things that make each country unique?

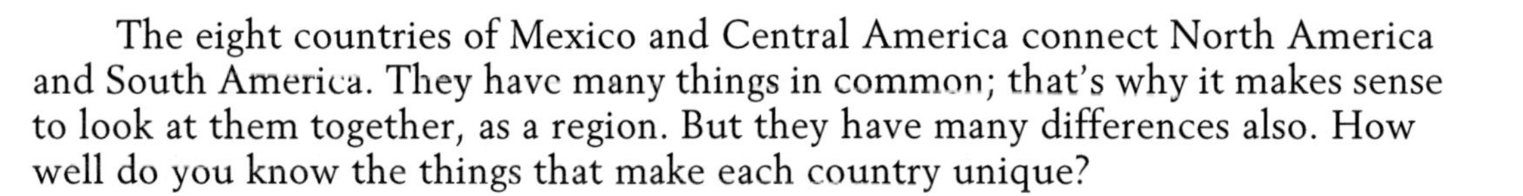

Each statement on this handout applies to only one of the eight countries of Mexico and Central America. Here are the names of the countries. Can you match each statement with the country it describes?

Belize	Costa Rica	El Salvador	Guatemala
Honduras	Mexico	Nicaragua	Panama

1. The quetzal, this country's national bird, has striking red and green feathers—some up to three feet long.
2. This sliver of land connects South America to Central America.
3. The currency is the Costa Rican colon.
4. Its capital is Guatemala City.
5. During the Day of the Dead fiesta in this country, people remember friends and relatives who have died.
6. Its currency is the colon.
7. Its currency is the Mexican peso.
8. Its currency is the balboa.
9. Its capital is Belmopan.
10. The Mayan city of Copan was built here somewhere between 1000 B.C. and A.D. 800.
11. This country joined the U.S. and Canada in NAFTA (the North American Free Trade Agreement).
12. Its currency is the cordoba.
13. Its capital is Panama City.
14. Its currency is the Belize dollar.

(continued)

Name ______________________________ Date ______________

Clues to the Region *(continued)*

15. The civilizations of the Mayas, Toltecs, and Aztecs helped shape this country's culture.
16. Central America's biggest population, largest city, and highest peak are all found here.
17. During the 1980's, Sandinistas and *contras* fought over how the country should be run.
18. English is the official language here.
19. Its capital is San Salvador.
20. Its capital is Mexico City.
21. Its capital is Tegucigalpa.
22. Its capital is San José.
23. A great river, the Rio Grande, separates this country from its neighbor to the north.
24. Its currency is the quetzal.
25. This country is the location of a famous canal.
26. This is the largest country in Central America.
27. This country is known for marimba music, played on an instrument like a xylophone.
28. This country was once a British colony.
29. Its currency is the lempira.
30. The capital of this country is Managua.
31. The national symbol shows an eagle perched on a cactus, holding a snake in one claw.
32. This is the smallest—and most densely populated—country in Central America.
33. Its name comes from the Spanish word for *depths.*

Economy and Trade in Mexico and Central America

Teacher Guide Page

OBJECTIVES

Social Studies

- Students will become familiar with some of the exports of the nations of Central America.
- Students will understand the connection between available resources and the economy.
- Students will differentiate among various forms of exchange and money.

Art

- Students will design and create currency.

Math

- Students will practice converting from one currency to another.

MATERIALS

Economy and Trade in Mexico and Central America handout
paper
pencils, colored pencils, markers, paints
scissors

BACKGROUND

One interesting twist sometimes arises in this simulation. Two countries both export the same item, but each assigns a different value to that item. Students may find this confusing and think that the same item should always have the same absolute value. Encourage them to realize that the same item can have a different value to different people, depending on its availability. Students should also be encouraged to look closely at the lists of items exported. Some countries have only a few exports; some have far more. Can students make any guesses about the economy of these countries, based on the amount of things they export? What about the types of things exported? Encourage students to speculate on the different economic strengths of a country like Mexico, which exports oil and petroleum products, and one like Honduras, which exports raw materials like wood, coffee, and bananas.

PROCEDURE

1. Distribute the handout and discuss it with students.
2. Model each stage of the activity. You can use either one of the currencies on the handout or the fictional currency given in the student procedure—the

minim, with an exchange rate of 10 to the dollar—and exports of oil, silver, and sugar.

3. Divide the class into groups. You can assign a country to each group, or you can allow students to choose their own countries.
4. Students should proceed as directed on the handout.
5. When all trades have been completed, have students look at the items listed under exports for each country. What kind of pattern do they see? (Several countries export coffee, sugar, bananas, cotton and other textiles, meat, shellfish.) What does this tell them about the economies of these countries? (Most of these items are food products; few are materials needed by industries in other countries. This suggests an economy largely dependent on agriculture, not industry.)

Variation

If time permits, have each group trade with a total of three other groups and then see how the goods they hold have changed. Do they still have any of their original goods? Did they receive any of their original goods back in a later trade? What is the monetary value of the goods they now hold based on the currencies of origin?

Assessment

Did students successfully carry out at least two transactions using Central American currency and export cards they created?

Extension Activity

These figures are based on the official rate of exchange as of April 1998. Since exchange rates change daily, these rates may be very different today. Have students research the current rates of exchange between each of these currencies and the dollar to see how much—or whether—they have changed.

Name ____________________ Date ____________

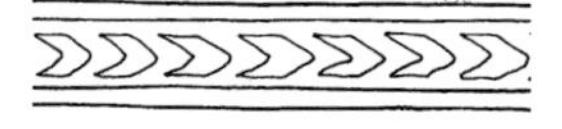

Economy and Trade in Central America

Like other countries around the world, the countries of Central America produce more than they need of some things. When they have a **surplus**, they can sell it to other countries as **exports**. The money they receive for these exports can be used to buy **imports**—things they need from other countries. However, most countries use different money systems. They have to work out how much one country's money, or **currency**, is worth in the other country's money before they can make a deal.

The table below lists the eight countries of Mexico and Central America. It shows each country's main exports. It also names the unit of money each country uses and the dollar exchange rate for that money. The dollar exchange rate is the amount of money you would have to give to equal one U.S. dollar. For example, if the dollar exchange rate were seven, you would have to pay seven units of that money to get a U.S. dollar. And, one U.S. dollar would buy seven units in that currency.

Your group will represent one of these countries.

Country	Currency	Exchange Rate (units/$US)	Main Exports
Belize	Belize dollar	2	timber, sugar, fish products, clothes, fruit
Costa Rica	Costa Rican colon	248.4	coffee, textiles, bananas, sugar, cocoa
El Salvador	colon	8.75	coffee, sugar, shrimp, flowers, textiles, corn, cotton
Guatemala	quetzal	6.25	coffee, sugar, bananas, beef, cotton
Honduras	lempira	13.3	coffee, bananas, timber, shrimp, lobsters, meat, sugar
Mexico	Mexican peso	8.5	petroleum and petroleum products, vehicles, engines, cotton, coffee, minerals, machinery, seafood
Nicaragua	cordoba	10.25	coffee, cotton, sugar, chemical products, meat, bananas
Panama	balboa	1	bananas, shrimp, coffee, sugar, textiles, petroleum products

(continued)

Name ______________________________ Date ______________

Economy and Trade in Central America *(continued)*

1. You have $100 worth of money in your currency. First, work out how many units of your currency you get for $100. (For example, if your currency was called the minim and your exchange rate was 10, you would have 10 minims for every dollar. Since you have a total of $100, you would have 1,000 minims.)

2. Now you need to create some bank notes so that you can buy things with the money. Decide what denominations you need in your currency. Will ones, fives, and tens work for your currency? Or do you need to start with hundreds and thousands?

3. Design and create bank notes for your currency. Each note should show the name of your country, the name of your currency, and the value of each note—one, ten, one hundred, and so on.

4. Now you need to create export cards for the items you export. The total value of your exports must equal the total value of your currency. Assign a value to each export card. (Again, let's suppose your currency is the minim and you export oil, silver, and sugar. You have a total of 1,000 minims. You might say that your oil was worth 500 minims, your silver was worth 400 minims, and your sugar was worth 100 minims, for a total of 1,000 minims.) Design and create cards for each item you export. Each card should show the name of the country, what the export is, and what the value of the item is.

5. Once you have money and things to export, it's time to get trading. Go to another group and make two exchanges with them. Buy one of their exports from them and sell them one of your exports. Convert your currency into their currency to make the sale. Don't worry if you can't match the currencies exactly because the units of your notes don't match; just get as close as you can.

6. Working in your group, write out the details of each transaction. Show your currency, the other group's currency, and how you converted from one currency to the other.

There's a Proverb That Says . . .

Teacher Guide Page

Objectives

Social Studies

- Students will understand some of the commonalities between different cultures.
- Students will understand that proverbs and sayings can be used to transmit culture.

Language Arts

- Students will analyze the meaning of unfamiliar phrases to find parallels with English phrases.
- Students will learn that proverbs can carry the wisdom of people from generation to generation.

Materials

There's a Proverb That Says . . . handout

Background

Proverbs are part of every spoken language. Comparing proverbs from various parts of the world shows that the same kernel of wisdom can be expressed in different ways. Proverbs often reflect the cultures that develop them. Many proverbs form part of a code of behavior that transmits rules of conduct within a culture. They also tend to use rhyme, alliteration, and homely imagery—household objects, animals, and the events of everyday life.

In North America the best-known use of proverbs is probably *Poor Richard's Almanack*, published annually by Benjamin Franklin from 1732–1757. Many of Franklin's proverbs were reworkings of old European proverbs with a colonial American twist.

Here are some Central American proverbs, with English equivalents:

El ejercicio hace el maestro. (Exercise makes a master.) Practice makes perfect.

Con lo que sana Susana, enferma Juana. (What heals Susana makes Juana ill.) One man's meat is another man's poison.

La mentira es como el maiz: sola sale. (Lies are like corn: They crop up by themselves.) Honesty's the best policy.

Procedure

1. Distribute the handout and discuss it with students. If you want, you can use some of the proverbs given in the Background section as examples while you model the process.
2. Students then proceed as directed on the handout. Encourage students to see how the Central American proverbs reflect culture.

Answers

1. *Quien bien va, no tuerce.* If it's going well, don't change it.
   If it ain't broke, don't fix it.
2. *De la mano a la boca se pierce la sopa.* Between hand and mouth the soup is lost. There's many a slip 'twixt cup and lip.
3. *Hombre prevenido vale por dos.* If a man is warned in advance, he is worth two. Forewarned is forearmed.
4. *Mas vale pajaro en mano que ciento volando.* A bird in the hand is worth more than a hundred flying. A bird in the hand is worth two in the bush.
5. *Quien pide no escoge.* The person who pleads does not choose.
   Beggars can't be choosers.
6. *Querer es poder.* To wish is to be able.
   Where there's a will there's a way.
7. *Tambien para los pinos hay hacha.* Even for pine trees, there's an ax.
   The bigger they come, the harder they fall.

Assessment

Were students able to identify similar proverbs in English, or at least to rephrase the Central American proverbs to sound like English ones?

Extension Activity

Have students choose a proverb to illustrate.

Name ______________________________ Date ______________

There's a Proverb That Says…

Proverbs are short, clever sayings. They use picturesque language to express a piece of wisdom. All cultures have developed proverbs, which in turn reflect the particular cultures they come from. For example, proverbs from the Sahara area may represent water as valuable, and proverbs from Southeast Asia may talk of crocodiles. Often, the same thought is expressed in proverbs from different cultures. For example, a Spanish proverb goes, "Cuantos hombres, tantos pareceres," or "So many men, so many minds." This means much the same as the English saying "It takes all kinds to make a world."

In some cultures people play a game with proverbs. The first player recites a proverb. The second player must think of a proverb that has a similar meaning and recite that.

Try playing a version of the proverb game with the following proverbs from Mexico and Central America. See if you can think of a proverb that means about the same thing as each of these. If you can't think of a proverb with a similar meaning, reword the proverb to sound like a familiar one.

1. *Quien bien va, no tuerce.* If it's going well, don't change it.

   ____

2. *De la mano a la boca se pierde la sopa.* Between hand and mouth the soup is lost. ______________________________

3. *Hombre prevenido vale por dos.* If a man is warned in advance, he is worth two. ______________________________

4. *Mas vale pajaro en mano que ciento volando.* A bird in the hand is worth more than a hundred flying.

   ____

5. *Quien pide no escoge.* The person who pleads does not choose.

   ____

6. *Querer es poder.* To wish is to be able.

   ____

7. *Tambien para los pings hay hacha.* Even for pine trees, there's an ax.

   ____

Central American Folktales

Teacher Guide Page

Objectives

Social Studies

- Students will recognize that different cultures express similar ideas in their literature.

English/Language Arts

- Students will examine some familiar features in Central American folktales.
- Students will create their own folktale.

Materials

Central American Folktales handout
writing materials
optional: trickster stories from other cultures

Procedure

1. This activity works best with two or three students working as a group on each folktale.
2. Distribute the handout, and discuss the concept of folktales and trickster stories. If you wish, share other trickster stories with students.
3. Have each group (or individual student, if you prefer) create its own trickster figure and develop a story around the figure.
5. When all stories are completed, students should present their stories orally to the class. Make copies of all stories for a classroom folktale anthology.

Variations

Have students research Central American trickster tales, choose one tale, and illustrate at least four scenes from the story. Display the illustrations in groups in the classroom.

Extension Activity

Have students illustrate their folktales.

Name ______________________________ Date ____________________

Central American Folktales

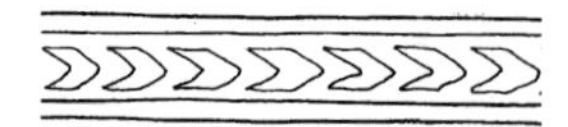

Many cultures developed stories about tricksters. The West African trickster Anansi has come into American culture as Brer rabbit. The Maya also had a rabbit trickster figure. In this story the trickster is tricked himself.

Once upon a time, the rabbit teamed up with the crab to grow carrots. They worked together for several days in harmony. First they chose the seed, and then they planted it. They took care of the young plants and weeded them. They harvested the crop and separated the leafy green tops from the carrots.

Rabbit was tempted to keep all the carrots for himself. He tried to fool the crab with sweet talk.

"Look, my friend, at the two piles we have there," he said. "One is big, but one is so small. I will be generous with you. You shall take the fine big pile, and I will take the small one."

The crab looked and saw that the big pile contained only the green tops of the carrots, while the small pile contained the carrots themselves, sweet and juicy. The crab answered, "Thank you very much, my dear friend, but I like to be fair. Let's divide the two piles in half and each take half. I will divide and you choose which half you want, or you can divide and I will choose, as you prefer. What do you say?"

But rabbit was greedy and wanted all the carrots for himself.

"No, no, I can't agree," said rabbit. "Let's decide it with a race. We'll walk over to that tree and then come back running. The first one to reach the pile of carrots can keep them, while the other gets the tops. What do you say?"

The crab thought for a moment before answering, "Well, all right, if that is your wish."

"Finally, we're in agreement!" said the rabbit. He was very happy, because he was sure he was going to win. When they got to the tree, the rabbit offered, "Now, since I know you're slower than I am, I'm going to give you a 10-pace head start."

(continued)

Name ______________________________ Date ______________

Central American Folktales *(continued)*

But the crab refused to accept the head start. "No, that's too much; I cannot accept," he said. "That would be taking advantage of you. In fact, you're the one who should have the head start. Please, I insist!"

The rabbit, eager to get the race over with, accepted the head start. He positioned himself in front of the crab and got ready to run. As soon as the rabbit turned his back on the crab, the crab seized the rabbit's tail with his claws, without the rabbit realizing it. The rabbit set off at top speed and soon came near the carrots. As he approached, he turned around to see how far behind the crab was. The crab let go of the rabbit's tail and dropped onto the pile of carrots.

The rabbit was surprised not to see the crab laboring along the path, so he called out, "Where are you, friend crab?"

"Right here," answered the crab behind him.

The rabbit jumped with surprise. He couldn't believe what he saw. There was the crab, climbing over the pile of carrots.

"Here I am," repeated the crab, "and I got here before you did."

This was the first time that anyone had ever beaten the rabbit at something. The rabbit had to accept that the crab had won, although he could not tell how it was done. And the crab was wise enough to keep silent about how he tricked the trickster.

The story of the rabbit and the crab reflects the culture that created it. What kind of character would a trickster have in your culture? Develop a trickster figure. Then write a story that involves the trickster. Illustrate your story, if you wish.

The Maya Codex

Objectives

Social Studies

- Students will explore some of the ways in which different cultures develop resources.

Math

- Students will apply precise measuring skills to the creation of an object.

Art

- Students will create and decorate a handmade paper book.

Materials

The Maya Codex handout
roll of unglazed white paper
lightweight card stock
decorated paper, or plain paper and materials to decorate it
rulers
pencils
construction paper
white glue

Preparation

Cut strips of 9" × 96" paper from the paper roll. Cut the card stock into $9\frac{1}{2}$" × $6\frac{1}{2}$" rectangles. Each book will require one paper strip and two pieces of card stock.

Procedure

1. Either distribute decorated paper, or give students plain paper and decorating supplies. Suitable materials include brushes and paint, collage materials, and simple printmaking materials like potato slices and cut erasers. Explain to students that they will be using this decorated paper for the front and back covers of their books, so they should make it as attractive as possible. (The Maya covered their codices with animal skin.)

2. Distribute the handout and go through the procedure with students. Stress that the measuring and folding step is critical. If all the segments of paper are not properly cut and all the folds are not absolutely straight, the finished book will be clumsy-looking and unattractive. Distribute materials. Students then proceed as directed on the handout.

Assessment

Did students produce a neat, accurately folded book?

Variation

Instead of creating a folded paper book, have students create an illustration of a scene from their lives in the style of Maya codex art. Figures were always shown in profile, heavily outlined in black. The captions, written in glyphs, ran above and below the figures.

Extension Activities

Have students use their folded books with the folktale activity on page 12 or the proverb activity on page 10. Once their writing is completed, they should carefully write their finished pieces in the folded book. Some pages can be used for drawings to illustrate the poems or folktale.

Bonus Question

Point out to students that they started off with a strip of paper 9" high and 96" long, and ended up with sixteen 6" × 9" pages. If they wanted a book with eight 8" × 10" pages, what size strip would they need to start off with? (10" × 64") What about a book with twenty 4" × 5" pages? (5" × 80") Would it be possible to make a book with 13 pages? Why not? (Because the last leaf on each end must face in the same direction to be attached to the covers. If the book had an uneven number of pages, the back cover couldn't be attached.)

Name ______________________________ Date ______________

The Maya Codex

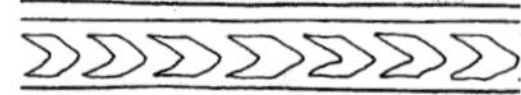

In Mexico and Central America today, many people are descendants of the **Maya**. From about A.D. 250 to A.D. 900, many Indian groups with common traditions and languages formed the Maya civilization. Maya territory stretched from Mexico to Honduras. In Europe, the Roman Empire was crumbling and a long Dark Age was beginning. In the Americas, the Maya were building great cities and making advances in science and astronomy. They developed a system of numbers that included the concept of zero, long before the idea came to Europe from India. They created a system of writing that combined symbols that stood for whole words and symbols that stood for sounds. These symbols—called "glyphs"—were used in many ways. They were carved in stone and painted in murals. They were also written on paper, in books.

Scholars are still trying to read Maya glyphs. They are being helped by speakers of modern Maya languages. Although the words have changed during the centuries since the classical Maya period, there is still enough of a resemblance to help scholars understand the ancient glyphs.

The Maya were among the early inventors of paper as a writing surface. To make paper, Maya artisans gathered bark from fig trees. They beat and softened the bark, then treated it with water and lime to get rid of the sap. In the next step the bark was flattened and dried. When it was fully dry, the bark peeled apart in sheets. The Maya folded these sheets together to form books. Unfortunately, the Spanish conquistadors destroyed all the Maya books they found. Only four of these books—called **codices**—survive today.

One of these surviving books is known as the Dresden Codex, because it is kept in Dresden, Germany. There are 39 leaves in the Dresden Codex. When the pages are all unfolded, it becomes a long accordion of paper—nearly 12 feet (3.5 m) long!

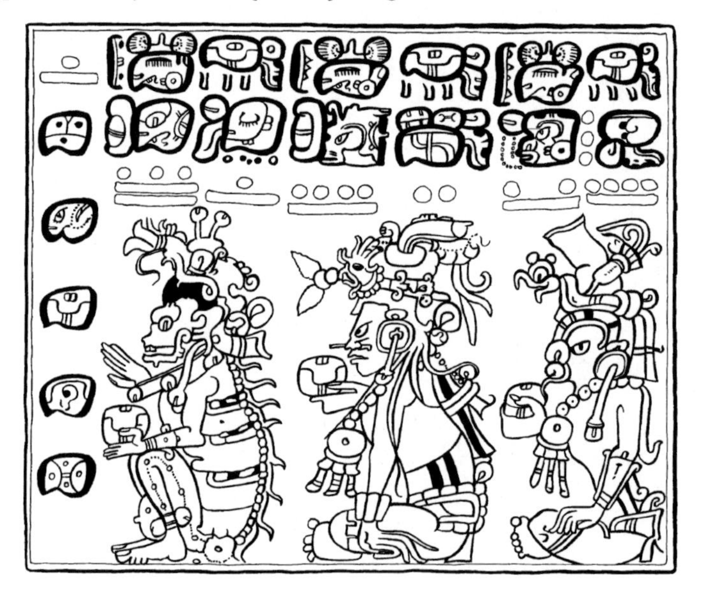

Page 13a of the Dresden Codex
The gods of death, maize, and the north (left to right), each holding the symbol for maize, are identified in the inscriptions above.

(continued)

Name ______________________________ Date ______________

The Maya Codex *(continued)*

These books are filled with pictures. Captions above and below the pictures are written in Maya glyphs. Some of the codices look a bit like an ancient comic strip, with the captions written above the picture in each frame of the strip. Themes include astrology, history, prophecy, and ritual. Gods, priests, rulers, and warriors were shown in profile and outlined in black.

You can make your own folded book in the style of Maya codices.

1. Fold your long paper strip every 6 inches, with one fold going forward and one going backward, like a fan. Accurate measuring and folding are important here. If any of your folds are crooked or if the pages aren't exactly the same size, the finished book will look sloppy.
2. To make a cover, take two pieces of $8\frac{1}{2}" \times 11"$ decorated paper. If your decorated paper is smaller than $8\frac{1}{2}" \times 11"$, glue the decorated paper to the center of a sheet of $8\frac{1}{2}" \times 11"$ construction paper. Place the decorated piece of paper face down on your work surface. Draw a straight line one inch from each edge. You should have a rectangle $6\frac{1}{2}" \times 9"$. Spread white glue on this inner rectangle. Carefully position one of the pieces of card stock on the glued area and press it in place. Cut off the corners of the decorated paper at a 45-degree angle.
3. Fold the edges of the decorated paper over the card stock and glue in place.
4. Place one cover at each end of the folded strip of paper. The pages should be centered on the height of the covers so that the covers stick out $\frac{1}{4}"$ above and below the pages. The back long edge of the folded paper—the spine of the book—should be even with the back edges of the covers. The front edge of the covers should stick out $\frac{1}{2}"$ beyond the pages.
5. Glue the first 6-inch panel of the folded paper to the inside of the front cover. Glue the last 6-inch panel to the back cover. Your bookmaking project is complete.

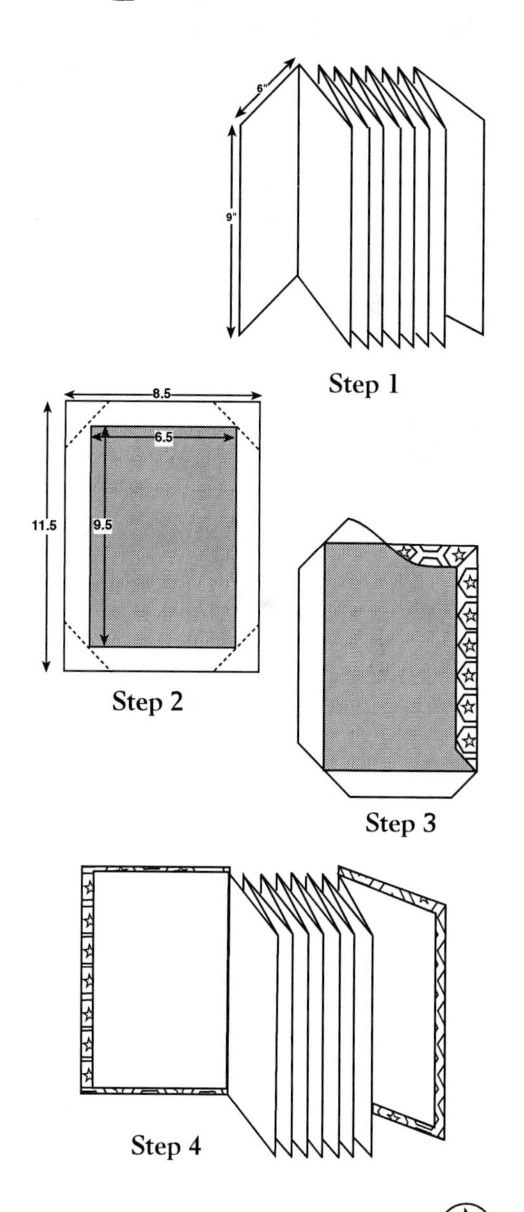

A Conversation in . . .

Teacher Guide Page

Objectives

Social Studies

- Students will be exposed to simple phrases in another language.
- Students will learn of some of the other languages spoken in Mexico and Central America before the Spanish Occupation.

Foreign Language/Spanish

- Students will learn everyday greetings in Spanish.
- Students will learn everyday greetings in Mayan.

Materials

Conversations in Central America handout
A Conversation in Mayan handout
A Conversation in Spanish handout
paper and pencils, scissors

Procedure

1. Distribute the handouts and discuss them with students. Can students identify any patterns in the Spanish or Mayan words?
2. Students proceed as directed on the handouts.
3. When students have had sufficient time to practice, choose one student from each of two different pairs to demonstrate their skills in Spanish/Mayan for the class. If time allows, have other student pairs recite their greetings in Spanish/Mayan.

Nahuatl Words

auakatl — avocado

chokolatl — chocolate

koyotl — coyote

tlaxkali — tortilla

tomatl — tomato

Assessment

Were students able to memorize simple phrases in Spanish/Mayan and combine them to form a conversation?

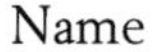

Name ______________________________ Date ______________

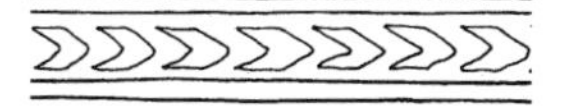

Conversations in Central America

What language do people speak in Mexico? In Honduras? In Belize? Many would answer, "Spanish. Everyone in these countries speaks Spanish." But, this isn't true. Hundreds of different languages—including Spanish—are spoken in Mexico and Central America.

When the Spanish first arrived in the Americas in the early 1500's, they encountered many different peoples and many different languages. The conquistadors needed interpreters to be able to communicate. As the conquerors started to set up an empire, they made Spanish the official language in the lands they took over. All the business of the colonial government was conducted using Spanish. Anyone who wanted to communicate with government officials needed to be able to speak Spanish. So, many Indians learned the new language.

However, just because they learned a new language, they didn't stop using their own languages. Millions of people still speak one or more Indian languages today. In Mexico, some two million people speak Maya, and another one million speak Nahuatl. Other Indian languages include Mixtec, Zapotec, Otomi, Totonac, Misquito, Lenca, and Jicaque, to name a few. There are probably about 800 different languages spoken in Latin America today. Many people who speak one of these languages also speak Spanish, but some speak only their native language—especially outside the cities.

Some words in English come from the native languages of Mexico and Central America. The words below are in Nahuatl, an important language in Mexico. Can you guess their meaning in English?

auakatl
chokolatl
koyotl
tlaxkali
tomatl

Hint: They are all words for things the Spanish had never seen before coming to America; four of these words are for foods that the Indians introduced to the Spanish.

Name ______________________________ Date ______________

A Conversation in Mayan

The Maya Empire once covered much of Mexico, Guatemala, and Belize, extending slightly into Honduras. The Maya made many scientific discoveries and left exquisite buildings and sculptures as part of their legacy. Although the empire is gone, many people in the region are still of Maya heritage. They even speak variants of the language of the Maya.

Here are some everyday phrases in Mayan. Working with a partner, prepare flash cards for these phrases. Practice saying them until you can hold a simple conversation in Mayan.

English	Mayan
Hello, how are you?	Bix a belex?
I'm fine, O.K.	Maloob.
Thank you.	Yum botic.
You're welcome.	Mixba.
Where are you going?	Tu'x ka binex?
I'm going home.	Kin bin tin nah.
Let's get going.	Koox tun.

Maya Pronunciation Tips

Written Mayan	Spoken Sound
a	*ah* as in *calm*
e	*eh* as in *effort*
i	*ee* as in *keen*
o	*oh* as in *open*
oo	same sound as *o*, but held longer
u	*oo* as in *moon*
x	*sh* as in *bush*

Name ______________________ Date ______________

A Conversation in Spanish

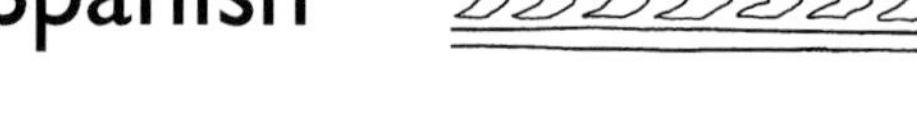

When Spaniards first arrived in Central America, hundreds of distinct peoples lived in the area. Each people had its own language. The coming of the Spaniards meant that the dominant language became Spanish. Even though the original, native languages of the different peoples are still spoken in many areas, Spanish is the official language of most countries in Central America.

In the box on the next page, you'll find some everyday phrases in Spanish. Working with a partner, prepare flash cards for these phrases. Practice saying them until you can hold a simple conversation in Spanish.

Spanish Pronunciation Tips

- Most Spanish words are stressed on the second-to-last syllable:
  ***gu**-sto; com-**pren**-do; **ha**-bla*
- Words that end in a consonant other than *n* or *s* are stressed on the last syllable:
  *us-**ted**; fa-**vor***
- The *h* is not usually pronounced in Spanish:
  habla sounds like *abla*
- *Ll* is pronounced like the *y* in *yes:*
  llamo sounds like *yamo*
- The letter *n* with a tilde—*ñ*—is pronounced like the *ni* in *onion:*
  mañana sounds like *manyana.*

Mexican vegetable vendors display their goods in the street.

(continued)

Name ______________________________ Date ______________

A Conversation in Spanish *(continued)*

English	Spanish
Hello.	Buenos días.
Goodbye.	Adiós.
Yes.	Sí.
No.	No.
Thank you.	Gracias.
You're welcome.	De nada.
Please	Por favor
Excuse me.	Perdón.
I do not understand.	No comprendo.
What is your name?	¿Cómo se llama usted?
My name is . . .	Me llamo . . .
Nice to meet you.	Mucho gusto.
The pleasure is all mine.	El gusto es mío.
How are you?	¿Cómo está usted?
I'm fine, thank you.	Muy bien, gracias.
Do you speak English?	¿Habla usted inglés?
Yes, I speak English.	Si, hablo inglés.

Mexican Tin Ornaments:

Teacher Guide Page

Objectives

Social Studies

- Students will understand the history of metalwork in Mexico before and after European colonization.

Art

- Students will create an ornament in the manner of Mexican tin ornaments.

Materials

Mexican Tin Ornaments handout
heavy aluminum foil (disposable baking trays work well), cut into 4-inch squares
paper and pencil for patterns
permanent marking pens
thread or ribbon for hanging
optional: examples of Mexican tin ornaments

Background

When the first Spaniards arrived in Mexico, they were amazed by the beautiful gold and silver ornaments of the Aztecs. An observer wrote, "When they were given these presents the Spaniards burst into smiles; their eyes shone with pleasure; they were delighted by them. They picked up the gold and fingered it like monkeys, they seemed to be transported by joy, as if their hearts were illuminated and made new. . . ."

To the Aztecs, gold and silver were precious because they were connected to the gods. Both gold and silver were reserved for priests, warriors, and high-ranking nobles. Aztec metalsmiths created ceremonial objects and offerings from the precious metals.

To the Spaniards, gold and silver were precious because of their innate properties. The Spaniards melted down the beautiful creations of the Aztec metalsmiths to get the pure metal.

Until the seventeenth century, a royal decree prevented Mexican Indian artisans from working with the precious metals of their country. When iron ore was imported, Indians were also debarred from using this more robust ore and from learning the new metalsmithing techniques coming from Europe.

Nevertheless, Mexican metalworkers persisted. When other metals were not available to them, they used tin—a soft, humble metal which Mexican artisans still transform into a myriad of shapes and forms today.

PROCEDURE

1. If you wish, you can begin by showing students examples of Mexican tin ornaments. Often used at Christmas time, the designs of these ornaments are not limited to Christmas themes. Point out to students that most of the ornaments have a fairly simple outer shape; the details are added with cut or embossed lines within the ornament.
2. Distribute the handout. Students proceed as directed to make their own versions of Mexican tin ornaments.
3. Display the completed ornaments in the classroom.

A Mexican tin ornament

Name ______________________ Date ______________

Mexican Tin Ornaments

Metalsmiths in Mexico work with many different metals. Gold is used to reproduce the ancient jewelry of the early Mixtecs, as well as for lacy filigree work. Mexican silverwork ranges from simple traditional motifs to elegant cast and embossed pieces. Copper, iron, and steel are used for jewelry, tools, and ornaments. And tin, a light and flexible metal, is used in any number of ways. Tin shops in Mexico are often filled with variety: embossed boxes, mirror frames surrounded by raised flowers, decorative trees full of birds and fruit. The metal is twisted, punched, cut, shaped, left plain, or painted in bright colors. Because it is so light, tin is ideal to use for hanging ornaments.

You can use heavy aluminum foil to make ornaments similar to Mexican tin ornaments.

1. First, choose a design for your ornament. Mexican tin ornaments include all kinds of objects: suns, stars, birds, animals, mermaids, houses, ships. To make cutting easier, simplify the outline of the shape. For example, the round curves of a butterfly's wings would be easy to cut, but long, thin antennae would be difficult. You can add plenty of detail later.

Step 2

2. Make a pattern drawing for your ornament. It should fit inside a 4-inch square. Remember, keep the outer shape simple. Within the outline, add details until you like the way your pattern looks.
3. Place your pattern on top of a piece of heavy aluminum foil. Trace over the lines of the design with a pen or pencil, pressing firmly. Any lines you make on the paper will be pressed into the foil underneath.

Step 4

4. Remove the pattern and cut around the outline of your ornament. Poke a hole for hanging. If any of the details need to be made clearer, go over the lines gently with a pencil. If you wish, use permanent markers to decorate your ornament.
5. Slip a length of thread or ribbon through the hanging hole and tie it to make a loop. Hang your ornament by the loop.

Cooking of Mexico

Teacher Guide Page

Objectives

Social Studies

- Students will see how geography can affect different aspects of culture.
- Students will become familiar with the essential components of Mexican cooking.

Materials

Cooking of Mexico handout
See individual recipes for materials for different dishes

Preparation

To save time, you may wish to do any slicing and chopping in advance.

Procedure

1. Distribute the handout about Mexican food and discuss it with the class. Encourage students to consider how the region's geography and climate—particularly rainfall—might affect the food people eat.
2. Divide the class into three groups, one for each recipe. Distribute the ingredients and recipe sheets to each group.
3. Students prepare the recipes as directed.
4. Once all the food is ready, gather around for a Mexican meal.

Name ______________________________ Date ________________

Cooking of Mexico

Mexico has given the world one of the most distinctive styles of cooking. Tomatoes, chocolate, vanilla, and peanuts are just a few of the foods that originally came from Mexico. They are now eaten all around the world.

Corn is the country's most important basic food. Since ancient times, corn has been used to make flat pancakes called *tortillas*. They are eaten like bread, made into a snack called *tacos*, or rolled around a filling for *burritos*.

Beans are another important ingredient in the Mexican diet, either eaten on their own or mixed with other ingredients. Beans are often used as a filling in *tacos* and in *burritos*. One of the Mexican dishes best known in this country, *chili con carne*, is made with meat, beans, chili peppers, onions, and spices.

Mexico has many other dishes that are not well known outside the country. One of these is *mole poblano*. It consists of chicken or turkey cooked in an elaborate sauce called *mole*. The *mole* is made up of 30 to 40 different ingredients—including unsweetened chocolate! Like many Mexican dishes, it represents a blend of Indian and Spanish cooking.

Throughout Mexico, tortilla and taco stands provide people with quick, freshly cooked meals at any time of the day. These are popular and bustling places at lunchtime, when they are filled with workers and shoppers.

Name ______________________________ Date ______________

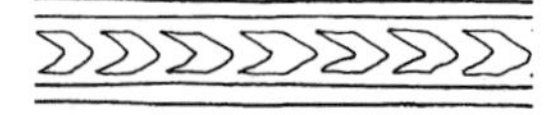

Cooking of Mexico: Arroz con Pollo (Rice with Chicken)

Ingredients

1 tablespoon vegetable oil

1 pound boneless, skinless chicken breasts, cut into thick strips

1 medium onion, chopped

1 medium green pepper, chopped

1 medium red pepper, chopped

1 clove garlic, minced

1 teaspoon chili powder

$\frac{1}{2}$ teaspoon ground cumin

$\frac{1}{4}$ teaspoon turmeric

$\frac{1}{2}$ teaspoon salt

$\frac{1}{2}$ teaspoon ground black pepper

1 cup uncooked rice

1 medium tomato, seeded and chopped

2 cups chicken broth

Yield: 4 servings

Procedure

1. Heat oil in a large skillet over medium heat Cook the chicken 8 to 10 minutes or until brown on all sides. Remove from pan.
2. Add onion, green pepper, red pepper, garlic, chili powder, cumin, salt, pepper, and turmeric. Cook 2 to 3 minutes or until vegetables are tender.
3. Add rice and tomatoes; stir until rice is lightly browned.
4. Add broth. Bring mixture to a boil, and place chicken pieces on top of mixture. Cover and simmer 20 minutes.
5. To serve, fluff with fork, stirring in chicken pieces.

Name ______________________________ Date ______________

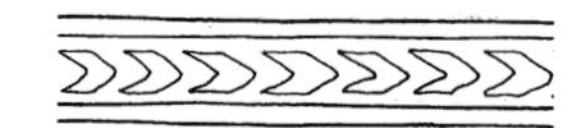

Cooking of Mexico: Arroz Dulce (Sweet Rice)

Ingredients	
1 cup rice	1 cup raisins
2 cups water	3 eggs, separated
$1/2$ cup sugar	$3/4$ teaspoon vanilla
1 teaspoon salt	$1/4$ teaspoon cinnamon
2 cups evaporated milk	$1/4$ teaspoon nutmeg
Yield: 4 servings	

PROCEDURE

1. Combine the rice, water, sugar, and salt in a large saucepan. Bring the water to a boil and cover the saucepan. Reduce the heat to low and continue to cook for 12–15 minutes, or until the water is absorbed.
2. Combine the milk and egg yolks. Add them to the rice. Then mix in the raisins, vanilla, and cinnamon. Simmer for 5 minutes. Remove from the heat.
3. Beat the egg whites until stiff. Fold them into the rice.
4. Chill. Garnish with nutmeg before serving.

Name ______________________________ Date ____________________

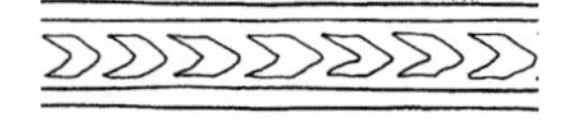

Cooking of Mexico: Bean Burritos

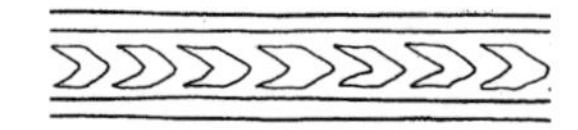

Ingredients

1 can (16 oz) light red kidney beans, drained

1 teaspoon vegetable oil

$\frac{1}{2}$ cup chopped onion

$\frac{1}{2}$ cup diced red *or* green bell pepper

1 clove garlic, minced

$\frac{3}{4}$ teaspoon ground cumin

$\frac{1}{2}$ teaspoon ground coriander

$\frac{1}{8}$ teaspoon white pepper

$\frac{1}{2}$ cup frozen whole kernel corn, thawed and drained

4 flour tortillas, 8 inches across

$\frac{3}{4}$ cup shredded cheddar cheese

1 cup medium salsa

baking sheet

Yield: 4 servings

Procedure

1. Preheat oven to 425°.
2. Place kidney beans in a small bowl. Mash to desired consistency.
3. Heat the oil in a small skillet over medium heat. Add onion, bell pepper, and garlic. Sauté 5 minutes or until onion is tender.
4. Stir in cumin, coriander, and white pepper. Cook one minute. Remove from heat.
5. Add onion mixture and corn to beans. Stir well.
6. Divide bean mixture evenly among tortillas, spreading to edges.
7. Sprinkle 3 Tbsp cheese down center of each tortilla.
8. Roll up tortillas. Place seam side down on a baking sheet. Bake at 425° for 5 minutes or until thoroughly heated.
9. Spoon salsa over burritos. Serve warm.

Panama: Molas

Teacher Guide Page

Objectives

Social Studies

- Students will understand that information about a region is not limited to written sources.
- Students will understand that art can provide a way of communicating and preserving historical events.
- Students will understand that art can help preserve the traditions and customs of a culture.

Art

- Students will understand some of the ways in which the history of a society affects its artistic development.
- Students will experiment with creating visual symbols for communication.
- Students will understand that art often uses symbols unique to the culture in which it is created.

Materials

Panama: Molas handout
paper, pencils, scissors, markers, glue sticks, and construction paper in a variety of colors
optional: examples of *molas*

Background

The Cuna Indians live on the San Blas Islands, off the coast of Panama. They have developed a striking reverse appliqué technique, known as *molas*. To make a mola, a Cuna woman stacks as many as seven layers of cloth together, a different color on each layer. She then draws a design on the top layer. The largest design elements are cut out, revealing the colors of the layers below. The cut edges are folded under and stitched down. The process continues with smaller elements cut from the layers. Eventually, all the large areas of color are broken up and filled with smaller shapes and lines.

Preparation

This activity can be done with fabric or with colored paper. Directions are given on the handout for making a paper mola. Simplified directions for making a fabric or felt mola are given under Variation, on the next page. The fabric gives a more authentic product, but the paper is easier to use.

PROCEDURE

1. Although this project can be successfully performed by individuals, it is also an excellent cooperative activity. Groups of three to five students work well.
2. Distribute the handout and discuss it with students.
3. Distribute materials. Model developing a pattern for a mola.
4. Most Cuna women use related colors to develop their molas. Encourage students to select analogous colors as they make their selections.
5. Display the completed molas in the classroom.

VARIATION

Cloth Molas

Materials

felt, fabric glue, needles and thread

Procedure

1. Develop steps 1 through 7 as with paper molas.
2. Do not glue paper mola pieces. Instead, use them as patterns to cut out felt pieces.
3. Assemble and stitch or glue felt pieces together. Begin by attaching the feature and/or detailed shapes to the basic silhouette.
4. Stitch the basic shape to the silhouette shape.
5. Stitch the silhouette shape to the base piece of felt.
6. Stitch background shapes.

A cloth mola design

Name ______________________________ Date ______________

Panama: Molas

The San Blas Islands lie off the shore of Panama. Among the people who live there are the Cuna Indians. About a hundred years ago, the Cuna developed a fabric-decorating technique called *mola.* In the Cuna language the word *mola* means "blouse." At first, the mola panels were used on the front of blouses. Today, *mola* refers to any fabric panels made by the Cuna Indians.

To make a mola panel, Cuna artisans layer different colors of fabric together. They then use appliqué and reverse appliqué techniques to create a design. The word *appliqué* comes from the French word for *applied.* To make a piece of appliqué, the artist cuts small shapes from fabric and applies them to a larger piece of cloth. To make reverse appliqué, the artist puts three or four layers of different colored fabrics together, then cuts a design through the layers and stitches the patterns to show the different layers of fabric. Embroidery stitches are used to add detail.

A variety of designs are used in creating molas. The Cuna often choose subjects that are part of their environment, such as fish, birds, animals, plants, and flowers. Sometimes they create geometric designs as well.

The background on most molas is suggested in a special manner. Long and short strips of fabric with rounded corners completely surround the design.

You can use colored paper to make your own version of a mola.

1. Begin by sketching two or three designs or drawings. Traditional designs using birds, animals, or fish make attractive molas. Geometric shapes, masks, plants, or flowers make good choices as well. Choose the best design to develop a mola.

2. Pick three colors of construction paper plus one sheet of black and one of white. The bottom layer serves as a base. It will remain a solid piece of paper.

Step 3

3. Cut out a silhouette shape of your basic drawing. Do not include any detail. **Do not glue any pieces until all patterns are cut out.**

(continued)

Name ______________________________ Date ______________

Panama: Molas *(continued)*

4. Cut out a silhouette shape slightly larger than your basic drawing. Now you have a basic shape surrounded by a larger silhouette.

5. Cut out features and detailed shapes. This step takes careful planning. Shapes should complement the basic shape.

6. Cut out and plan background shapes.

7. Carefully glue assembled pieces to the base piece of paper.

Step 4

Step 5

Steps 6 and 7

Appellidos: Getting the Name Right

Teacher Guide Page

Objectives

Social Studies

- Students will understand some of the commonalities and differences among naming ceremonies and traditions in different cultures.

Materials

What's in a Name? handout
pencil and paper

Background

In Spanish-speaking countries married women usually keep their maiden names. The husband's surname—often preceded by *de* (of)—is added to the wife's name. For instance, Liliana Guadalupe Escobar Hernandez has four official names. The first two are hers alone. The third name—Escobar—is her father's surname; it was also his father's family name. The fourth name—Hernandez—is her mother's family name. If Liliana were to marry a man named Oscar Hurtado Gomez, she would take the first part of his surname—Hurtado—and use it instead of her mother's family name, thus becoming Liliana Guadalupe Escobar Hurtado.

Procedure

1. Distribute the handout and discuss it with students.
2. Students proceed as directed on the handout.

Answers

1. Ojeda Ortega
2. Ogazon Vasquez
3. Barrionuevo Alarcon
4. Ferrete Gamero
5. Belloso Delgado
6. Aramayo Carrero
7. Pérez Lastra

Name ______________________________ Date ______________

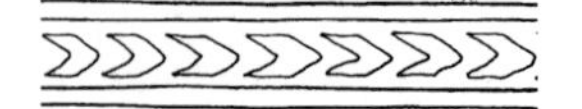

Appellidos: Getting the Name Right

In Anglo-American tradition, when a couple marries, the wife takes her husband's surname (last name). Any children they have are given the husband's surname. Although many women today don't take their husband's name, their children are often given the father's surname.

In other cultures, naming traditions are often different. Mexican surnames are based on the Spanish tradition. Mexicans usually use two "last names"—the surnames of both the mother and father. The father's last name is placed before the mother's last name. So Marta Carrera Lopez is the daughter of a man named Carrera and a woman named Lopez. Julio García Alvarez is the son of a man named García and a woman named Alvarez. When two people marry, the woman keeps the first part of her surname and adds the first part ofher husband's surname. The word "de," meaning "of," is usually added between the two names. If Julio García Alvarez and Marta Carrera Lopez were to marry, Marta would not become Marta García Alvarez, but Marta García de Carrera. Their children might be Lupe and Paco García Carrera.

If the following people married, what would their children's surnames be?

1. Dolores Ortega and Carlos Ojeda: ______________________
2. Graciela Vazquez and Tonio Ogazon: ______________________
3. Inés Alarcon and Eduardo Barrionuevo: ______________________
4. Luisa Gamero and Miguel Ferrete: ______________________
5. Sara Delgado and Andrés Belloso: ______________________
6. Bárbara Carrero and Paco Aramayo: ______________________
7. Mónica Lastra and Héctor Pérez: ______________________

What naming tradition does your family use? If your family used the Mexican tradition, what would your last name be?

Music in Central America

Objectives

Social Studies

- Students will understand how music contributes to the development and transmission of culture.
- Students will compare the ways in which different groups of people address the same concerns.
- Students will see that culture is an integrated whole and that language, literature, the arts, traditions, beliefs, and values all interact to form it.

Music

- Students will understand the importance of traditional Central American instruments.
- Students will make their own simple musical instruments.

Art

- Students will make and decorate a clay flute.

Materials

Music in Central America handout
self-drying clay
water
knife
large needle
poster paints, water-based sealer

Procedure

1. Distribute the handout and discuss it with the class.
2. If you wish, divide students into groups. Students proceed as directed on the handout.

Name ______________________________ Date ______________

Music in Central America

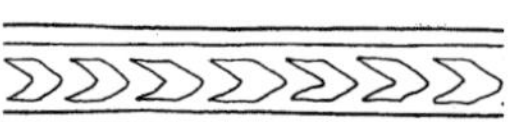

Long ago, people discovered they could make pleasant sounds by blowing air against a sharp edge. This caused the edge to vibrate. The musical instruments that use this principle are called **aerophones**. They range from plain penny whistles to the grandest church organ. Many aerophones were developed by the Maya in Mexico and Central America. Some were simple whistles. Some were multiple flutes of three or four pipes. Blown from a single mouthpiece, the pipes sounded chords.

You can make a simple clay flute, like those made by the Maya 2,000 years ago.

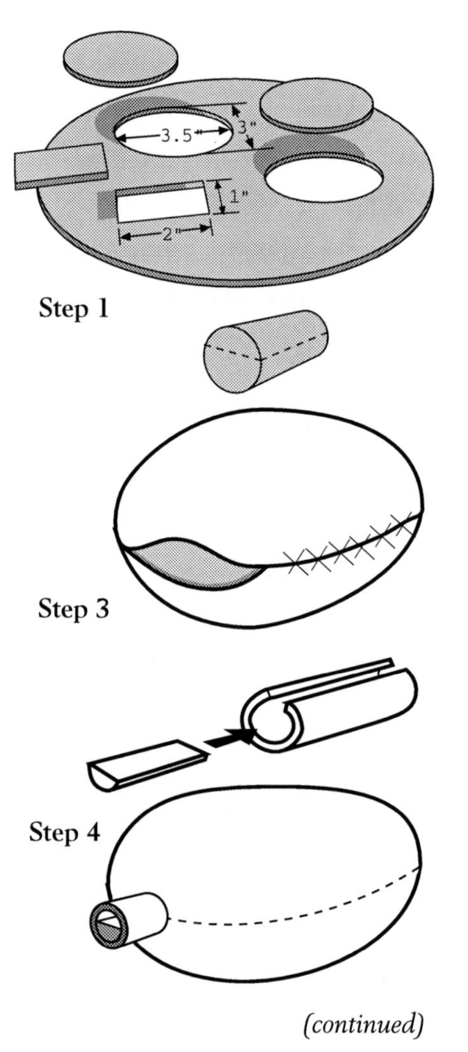

1. Roll a piece of clay flat. Cut out two egg shapes, $3 \times 3\frac{1}{2}$ inches (7×9 cm). Cut out a rectangle 2×1 inch (5×2 cm). Roll the clay rectangle up into a 1-inch (2 cm) log. Cut a thin slice off the long side of the roll.

2. Score the edges of each piece of clay with a large needle. Moisten the edges with water.

3. Form each egg into a bowl shape. Press the two shapes carefully together to form a hollow egg. This is the body of your flute. Score the edges together with the needle, leaving a gap at one end. Smooth the joint with a little water.

4. Form the clay rectangle into a short tube. Attach it to the opening in the flute by scoring. Push the clay roll into the tube, flat side up, leaving a gap to blow through. Smooth the clay with dampened fingers.

(continued)

Name ______________________ Date ______________

Music in Central America *(continued)*

5. Use the needle to make four small holes in the upper surface of the flute.

6. Make one larger hole on top, just behind the blowing hole.

7. Make two small holes in the lower surface of the flute.

8. Check that the flute works before it dries hard. Holding it carefully, cover the four small holes with your fingers. Gently blow through the end hole. If the flute does not whistle, adjust the edge of the large hole with your fingers. (The sound is made by blown air hitting the far edge of this hole.)

9. Leave the flute to dry. Paint with poster paints. Seal with water-based sealant.

Steps 5 and 6

Step 7

Step 9

Nearika: Yarn Paintings

Teacher Guide Page

Objectives

Social Studies

- Students will see how a visual art can be used to transmit culture.

Art

- Students will create a yarn painting.

Materials

Nearika: Yarn Paintings handout
pencils and paper
scissors
glue
8" × 10" or 10" × 12" heavy illustration board
four-ply yarn in bright colors
toothpicks or nails
optional: examples of Huichol yarn paintings

Background

The Huichol Indians live deep in Mexico's Sierra Madre. The rugged landscape has helped the Huichols resist outside influences. They remained unconquered by the Spanish until well into the eighteenth century. Even then, the Huichols kept their traditional religion and mythology.

Many Huichol arts and crafts have a religious connection, including the *nearikas*, or yarn paintings. Traditional nearikas are made either to express something seen in a vision or as a prayer offering to the gods. For example, images of serpents, waves, or water gourds express a wish for rain. Yarn paintings made to sell outside the area appear to include many of the same subjects as traditional nearikas, but in these paintings, the motifs are arranged for aesthetic reasons only. They are not intended to express either a vision or a prayer.

Procedure

1. Distribute the handout and discuss it with students.
2. Distribute paper and pencils. Have students start out with realistic sketches, then turn them into stylized versions. Model developing a stylized version of a realistic drawing.
3. Distribute materials. Students proceed as directed on the handout. Display completed nearikas in the classroom.

Variation

Some yarn paintings are made into decorative useful items, such as vases. Have students create yarn paintings to cover a bowl, box, vase, or other item.

Name ______________________________ Date ______________

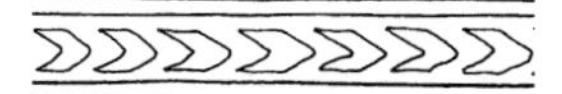

Nearika: Yarn Paintings

The Huichol Indians are descendants of the Aztecs. They live in the mountains of Nayarit in north central Mexico. One of their traditions includes making colorful yarn paintings called *nearikas.* A board is covered with soft beeswax, warmed in the sun. Then lengths of yarn are pressed into the soft wax to make a picture. Authentic nearikas are complex pictures of visions.

The word *nearika* means "countenance." Nearikas show the face of the wind, of the sun, of corn—any of the forces and beings that surround us. These natural subjects are simplified and stylized, then created in yarn.

Yarn paintings are made for two reasons. The first one is religious. They are made by Huichol men from visions they have had. The yarn paintings based on these experiences are sacred and rarely leave the area. The second reason nearikas are made is for sale. The Huichols and other Indians make yarn paintings for tourists and specialty shops. Almost all subjects are found in these nearikas.

You can make a simplified version of a nearika using yarn and glue.

1. The sun, plants, birds, or animals are all good choices for Huichol-style paintings. Sketch two or three ideas and pick one you like best. Transfer the design to heavy cardboard.

Step 1

(continued)

Name ______________________________ Date ______________

Nearika: Yarn Paintings *(continued)*

2. Spread a thin layer of glue around the edge of the board. Cut a length of yarn long enough to go all the way around the edge. Twist the end of the yarn to keep it from fraying. Starting at one corner, press the yarn into the glue around the edge of the painting. Keep the corners straight. Twist the ends of the yarn at the beginning and end of each yarn strand. Make a border of one or two strands of yarn. Be careful not to let the yarn curl or overlap. You may want to use a toothpick or pencil to guide the string.

Steps 2 and 3

3. With yarn, outline the design you have drawn in the same way as you did the border.

4. With a pencil, lightly section off the design. Then, fill in with glue and yarn one section at a time. Try to keep the yarn strands close together.

5. After you finish the design portion, fill in the background. Again, section off the background, as you did the design. Spread the glue lightly over one area at a time, and fill with yarn.

Steps 4 and 5

Tree of Life

Objectives

Social Studies

- Students will understand how religious beliefs affect art.

Art

- Students will create a tree of life.

Materials

for each student or group of students:
Tree of Life handout
self-hardening clay
three pieces of heavy cardboard
low, wide tin can
dowels
florist's wire
craft knife
glue
pliers
wire cutters
poster paints and brushes
epoxy glue
water-based sealant
optional: photographs or examples of Mexican Trees of Life

Procedure

1. Distribute the handout and discuss it with the class. If you wish, divide students into groups.
2. Students proceed as directed on the handouts.
3. Display the completed trees in the classroom.

Variation

If students have access to a kiln, have them make Trees of Life using clay only, to come closer to the traditional Tree of Life.

Name ________________________________ Date ____________________

Tree of Life

Colorful and ornate, the Trees of Life from Metepec are famous throughout Mexico. The theme, which originated in the Middle East, was brought to Spain by the Moors. In Spain, the Tree of Life took on a Christian significance. It commemorates the Creation, when Adam and Eve knew perfect happiness in the Garden of Eden. Introduced into Mexico after the Spanish Conquest, the Tree of Life became popular with the potters of Metepec in the state of Mexico. They create elaborate candle holders out of clay, ranging in size from tiny to enormous.

Traditionally, the Tree of Life is made entirely out of clay. You can make a simplified version by using a cardboard support for the clay.

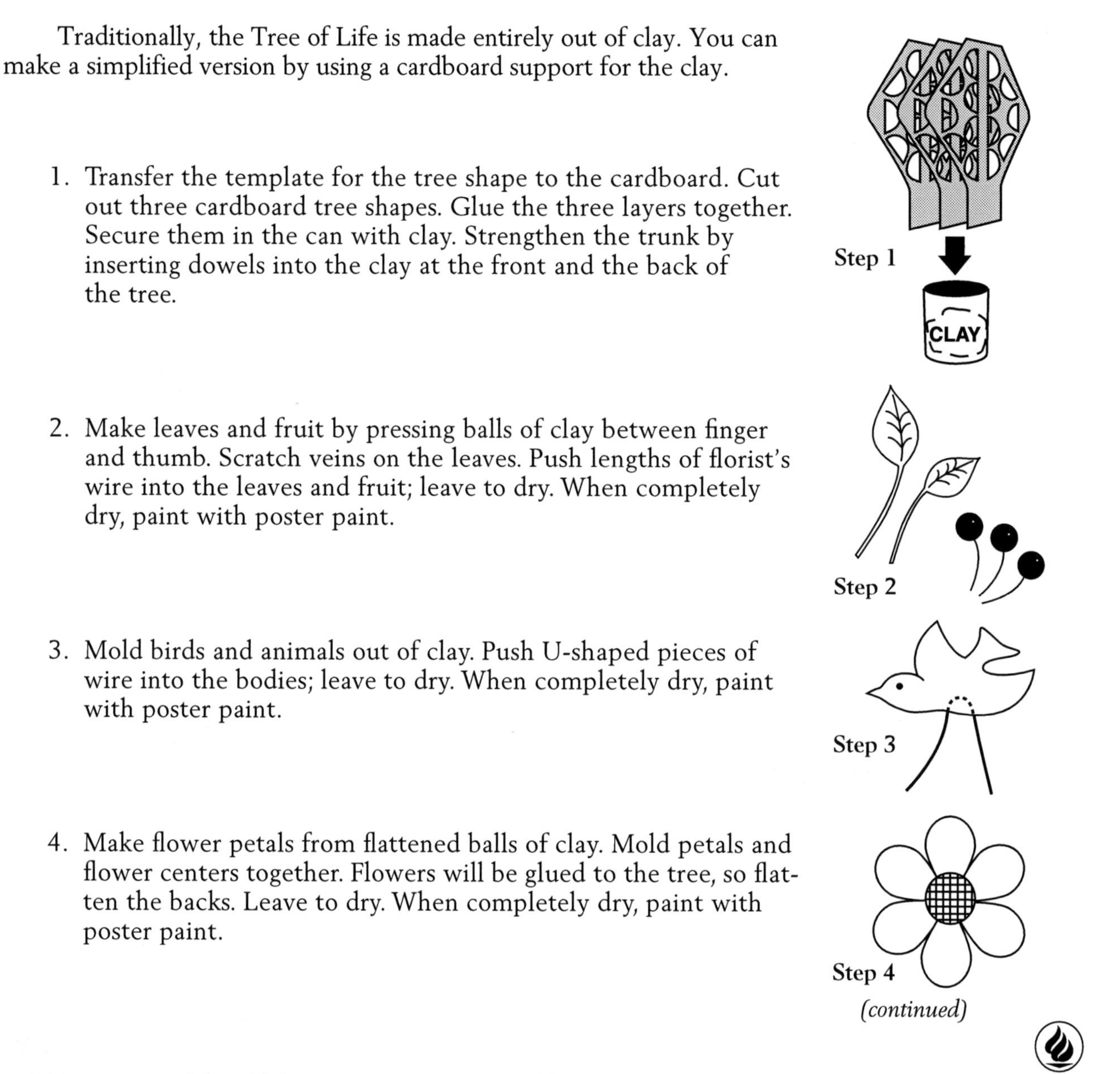

1. Transfer the template for the tree shape to the cardboard. Cut out three cardboard tree shapes. Glue the three layers together. Secure them in the can with clay. Strengthen the trunk by inserting dowels into the clay at the front and the back of the tree.

2. Make leaves and fruit by pressing balls of clay between finger and thumb. Scratch veins on the leaves. Push lengths of florist's wire into the leaves and fruit; leave to dry. When completely dry, paint with poster paint.

3. Mold birds and animals out of clay. Push U-shaped pieces of wire into the bodies; leave to dry. When completely dry, paint with poster paint.

4. Make flower petals from flattened balls of clay. Mold petals and flower centers together. Flowers will be glued to the tree, so flatten the backs. Leave to dry. When completely dry, paint with poster paint.

(continued)

Name ______________________ Date ______________

Tree of Life *(continued)*

5. Starting at the bottom of the tree, cover the cardboard shape generously with clay. Round and smooth the branches as they are covered.

6. Attach birds, leaves, and fruit while covering the tree skeleton. Hold in place with one hand, and twist the wire around to the back of the branch. Cover the wires with clay to secure.

7. Roll strips of clay for candle holders and attach to the tree. Allow the tree to dry.

8. To attach flowers, lay the dried tree flat on crumpled newspaper. Attach the flowers with epoxy glue. Allow glue to dry.

9. Touch up paint as necessary, and add details if desired. Seal the tree with water-based sealant.

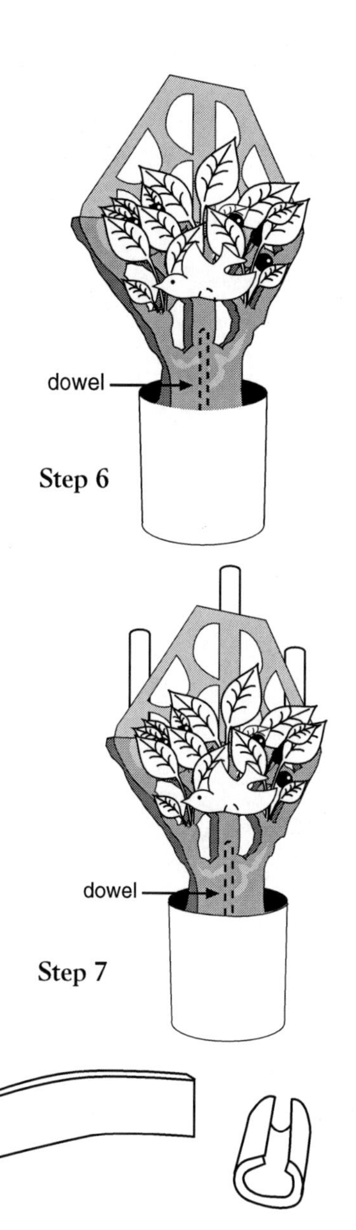

Name ______________________ Date ______________

Tree of Life *(continued)*

Tree of Life Template

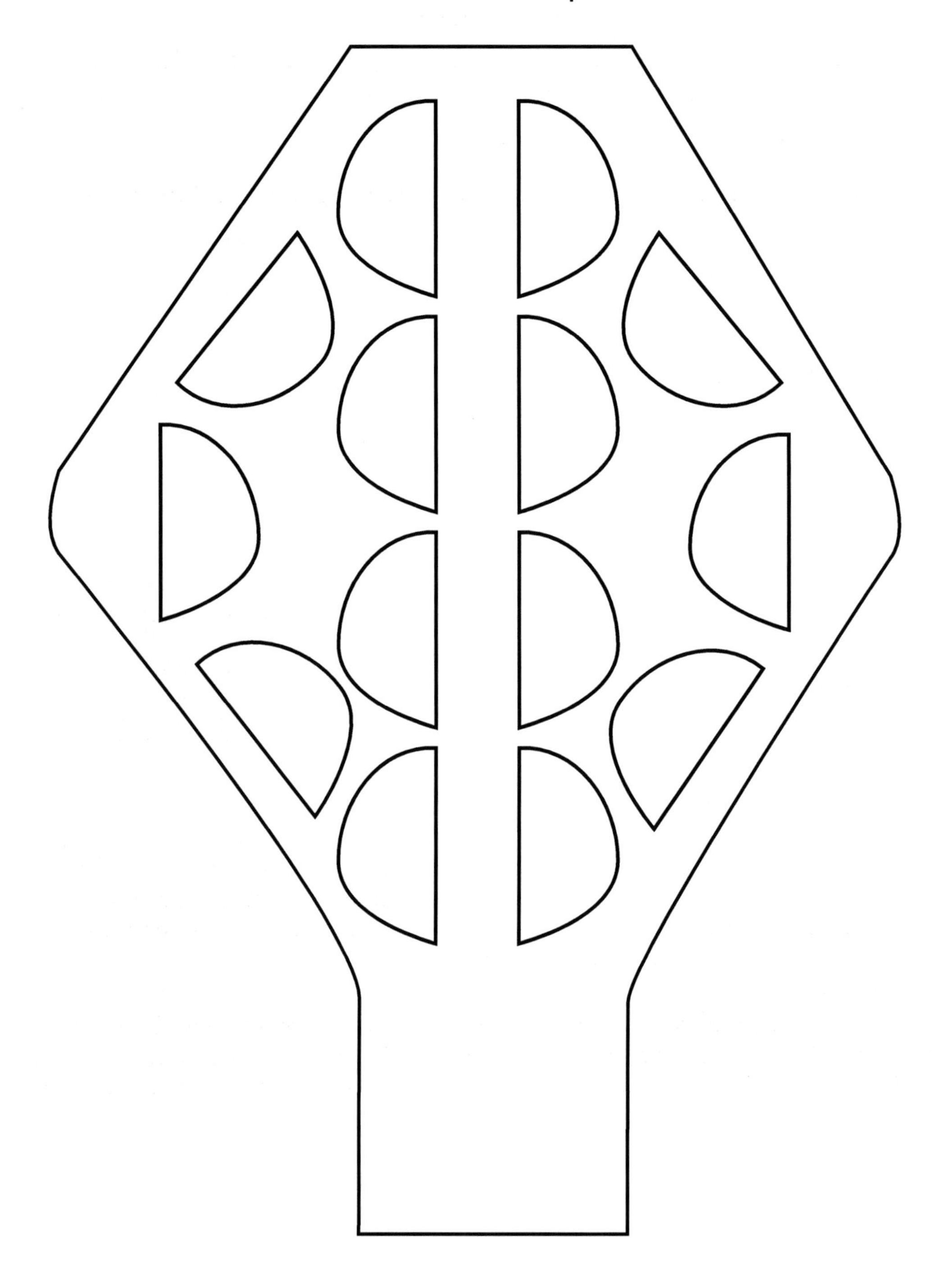

Day of the Dead

Teacher Guide Page

OBJECTIVES

Social Studies

- Students will understand the historical origins of a modern festival.
- Students will become familiar with some Mexican attitudes toward death.

Art

- Students will model a figure in clay in the manner of Mexican *calaveras* figures.

MATERIALS

Day of the Dead handout
self-drying clay
tempera paints
cotton wool
glue
optional: examples or photographs of Mexican calaveras figures

BACKGROUND

For the Aztecs of ancient Mexico, life and death were two sides of the same reality. The sun set every day, only to rise again. People died, and other people were born.

This attitude to death is still seen today in the Day of the Dead festivities. Skulls and coffins are not grim reminders of the inevitable end of life; they are reminders of the spirits of loved ones who are allowed to return on this one day of the year.

In preparation for the Day of the Dead, families tidy up graveyards. In some areas the graves are decorated with wreaths of marigolds—*las flores de los muertos,* "the flowers of the dead." Candles are lit to guide the spirits of the dead. In homes and offices, *ofrendas,* or tables covered with food and decorations, are prepared for the dead souls. Incense is burned on the ofrenda; since the dead take only the scent of the offerings, a strong scent is important.

In some areas, the Festival of the Dead begins on October 28, with a day set aside for los accidentados, those who have died in accidents. October 31 is set aside for dead children; their spirits withdraw on November 1, All Saints's Day, as the spirits of the adults arrive. These spirits can stay until November 2, All Souls' Day; then all the souls depart for another year.

Procedure

1. Distribute the handout and discuss it with the class. If you wish, show students photographs or examples of calaveras.
2. Students proceed as directed on the handout.
3. Display the completed figures in the classroom.

Extension Activity

Instead of celebrating Halloween, have a Day of the Dead celebration in the classroom, with students' calaveras figures part of the display.

Name ________________________________ Date ________________

Day of the Dead

Throughout the year, people in Mexico have holidays and festivals. Some holidays, like Constitution Day (February 5) and Revolution Day (November 20) commemorate events from history. Some holidays, like Los Santos Reyes (The Holy Kings, January 6) or Christmas Day (December 25) observe Christian feasts. But people in Mexico have one festival that is based on an Aztec festival: el Dia de los Muertos—the Day of the Dead.

The Day of the Dead is celebrated from November 1 to November 2. On this date, for 24 hours, the spirits of the dead are allowed to visit their friends and relatives on earth. Families prepare special altars, call *ofrendas*, to welcome the spirits of the dead. These altars are decorated with marigolds, which the Aztecs considered sacred to the dead. They are covered with photographs and offerings of food and fruit.

Miniature widow of painted clay

This description may make the Day of the Dead sound like a sad occasion. In Mexico, it isn't. This really is a festival, a celebration of life. In shops and markets all over Mexico, special items are sold for the Day of the Dead. Bakeries make bread in the shape of skulls, skeletons, and other symbols of death. Skulls of colored sugar are decorated with people's names. Shop windows are filled with items to celebrate the Day of the Dead. There are elaborate wooden scenes, brightly painted, with moving parts: turn a handle and skeletons turn slowly on a merry-go-round, or kick up their heels in a church. Toy makers offer papier-mâché skulls with movable lower jaws, and cardboard skeletons that dance at the pull of a string. They also sell ***calaveras***—tiny skeleton figures shown fully clothed, doing everyday things. There are skeleton brides marrying skeleton grooms, skeleton footballers, skeleton policemen—even skeletons on their knees at the graves of dead friends!

These strange little figures are usually made of painted clay. Cotton-wool "hair" is glued to their heads. Often, other details are also glued on: a bit of lace for a veil, a bouquet of tiny paper flowers.

You can make your own calaveras figure like the ones made in Mexico.

1. Decide on a scene for your calavera. You can include a single figure or a group.
2. Model your figure from self-hardening clay. Include the figure's clothes. As you model the face, remember that this is supposed to suggest a skeleton. You want to show the bones underneath the skin, not the skin itself. Leave the figure to dry.
3. When your figure is completely dry, paint on clothes and details. Glue on cotton-wool hair. Your calavera is ready for the festival!

Wooden Toys

Teacher Guide Page

Objectives

Social Studies

- Students will understand some of the common features of playthings from different cultures.

Art

- Students will create a simple toy.

Materials

Wooden Toys handout
stiff card or thin plywood
lengths of dowel or bamboo
glue
paint
drill
string

Preparation

If you want students to make wooden toys, animal bodies should be cut out in advance using a jigsaw or coping saw.

Procedure

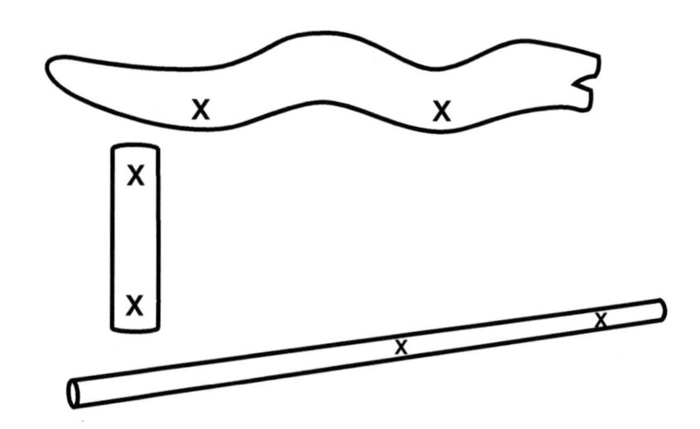

1. Distribute the handout. Students proceed as directed on the handout.
2. When students have made the bodies and legs of their toys, drill holes in the bodies, legs, and dowels as shown in the diagram.
3. You may want to model the procedure for attaching the legs and bodies with string.

Name ______________________ Date ______________

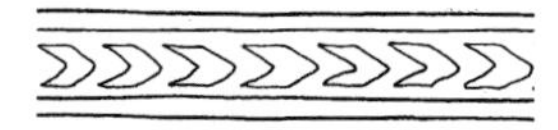

Wooden Toys

All around the world, children and adults create toys from the materials around them. In Mexico, traditional toys are made of many materials—wood, clay, papier-mâché, metal, and fabric. Some toys are associated with a particular festival. The whirring noise of fish- or bird-shaped *matracas* accompanies Easter celebrations. Miniature coffins and skulls appear for the Day of the Dead. Other toys, like these jointed animals, are found all year long.

Traditionally, these simple toys are made from pieces of fruit crates. You can make your own—less sturdy—versions from stiff card.

1. Design the body of an animal for your toy, and draw a pattern. Trace the pattern three times onto the stiff card, and cut them out. Glue the three pieces together in layers to form the body of your toy.
2. Draw a pattern for your toy's legs. Cut it eight times out of the cardboard. Glue two layers together for each of the four legs.
3. Use poster paint to paint your toy.
4. Tie a knot in one end of a length of string. Pass the string through the top of one leg so that the knot is pulled up against the outside of the leg. Then pass the string through the body and through the top of a second leg. Knot the end of the string.
5. Repeat step 4 for the other pair of legs.
6. Tie a knot in one end of a length of string. Pass the string through the bottom of one leg so that the knot is pulled up against the outside of the leg. Then pass the string through the stick and through the bottom of the opposite leg. Knot the end of the string.
7. Repeat step 6 for the second pair of legs.
8. To use your toy, hold the long end of the stick. Move it back and forth to make your animal dance.

Steps 1 and 2

Steps 4 and 5

Steps 6 and 7

The Mexican Mural Tradition

Objectives

Social Studies

- Students will learn that history can be expressed through the visual arts.
- Students will learn about the history of the mural tradition in Mexico.

Art

- Students will use a visual medium to present a narrative.
- Students will be exposed to the work of Diego Rivera.
- Students will create a mural painting.

Materials

The Mexican Mural Tradition handout
large sheet of paper
pencils and paints
slides or reproductions of murals by Diego Rivera
optional: reproductions of pre-Columbian murals

Procedure

1. Distribute the handout. Show students slides or reproductions of the murals of Diego Rivera.
2. Divide students into groups. If you like, assign each group a subject for their mural. Murals can be independent or can function together to narrate a history, as Diego Rivera's murals often did.
3. Students proceed as directed on the handout.
4. Display the completed murals in the classroom.

Variation

Many of Diego Rivera's murals were in fact frescoes—that is, they were painted on wet plaster, so that the paint and the plaster bonded as they dried. Use a shallow foil or plastic container to pour a slab of plaster for each student. Students can paint a fresco on the slab using tempera paint. If the fresco cannot be completed in one session, keep the plaster damp by wrapping it in a damp cloth until the next session. (Sheetrock™ does not make a good substitute for plaster, as it is coated with paper on both sides.)

Extension Activity

Rivera was one of a group of Mexican artists who developed a new approach to mural painting. Other artists included José Clemente Orozco (1883–1949), David Siqueiros (1898–1974), and Rufino Tamayo (1899–). Have students research the work of these other important Mexican mural painters.

Name ______________________________ Date ______________

The Mexican Mural Tradition

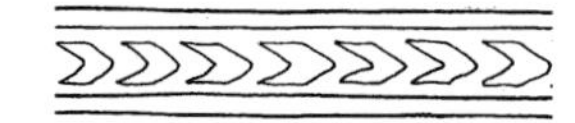

Murals—paintings on walls—have a long tradition in Mexico. The Maya painted murals on the stone walls of their temples. These murals showed scenes from myths, as well as scenes from real life.

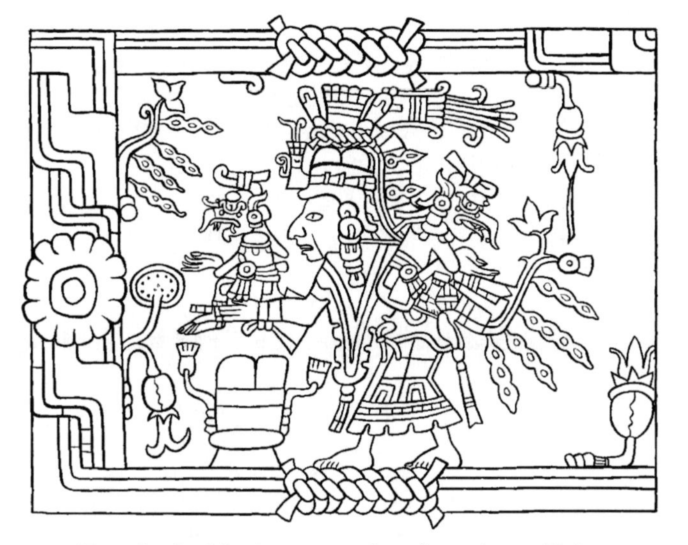

Detail of a Mexican mural at the ruins at Tulum

In the early twentieth century, this mural tradition was revived by some of Mexico's finest artists. Diego Rivera was one of them. Rivera was born in Mexico in 1886. As a boy, he loved to draw. As he grew older, he began to study at the San Carlos Academy of Fine Arts. He was expelled from the school after taking part in a student riot. After that, Rivera went to Europe to study art.

In the early 1900's, the traditional European style of painting was copied in other parts of the world, including Mexico. Mexican artists studied this style and used it to paint portraits and landscapes. When Rivera went to Europe, he discovered other ways of painting. He saw the works of Pieter Breughel, a painter who had worked in northern Europe centuries earlier. Breughel's paintings weren't stiff, conventional paintings of rich people. They showed lively village scenes, with country people working, dancing, eating. They gave a believable picture of real people. Another painter who influenced Rivera was the French painter Paul Cézanne. Cézanne's paintings were full of color and movement. They created a strong feeling of the French countryside.

Rivera realized that he didn't want to paint in the European style. He wanted to create a Mexican style of painting, a style that reflected the roots and culture of his people.

(continued)

Name ______________________ Date ______________

The Mexican Mural Tradition *(continued)*

When he returned to Mexico in the early 1920's, Rivera began to paint murals. The people in his paintings are solid, almost massive. The murals tell the history of the Mexican people. He painted the legend of Quetzalcoatl, an ancient Aztec god. He painted the coming of the Spaniards and their conquest over the Aztecs. He painted scenes that showed the growth of independence in Mexico.

In 1932, Diego Rivera was commissioned to paint murals for the Detroit Institute of the Arts. One of the murals, "Vaccination," was attacked. Some people thought it was a caricature of the Christian Holy Family. The next year, Rivera did a mural for Rockefeller Center in New York called "Man at the Crossroads." It created an uproar. One of the figures in the mural looked like the Communist leader Lenin. The mural was chipped from the wall and reassembled at the Palace of Fine Arts in Mexico City.

You can use mural painting to tell a story, as Diego Rivera did.

1. Your teacher may assign a topic for your mural, or you can choose a story yourself. Decide on the main topics of the story. How can you show these elements visually so that other people can understand what you are trying to express? Work with your group to develop a layout for your mural.

2. Draw in the scenes of your mural. When you have all the elements positioned, paint the mural.

Shopping in Mexico: The Tiangui

OBJECTIVES

Social Studies

- Students will learn about the market, a Latin American economic institution.
- Students will demonstrate the concepts of bargaining and exchange.

Art

- Students will design and create currency.

Math

- Students will bargain for purchases in a foreign currency.

MATERIALS NEEDED

Shopping in Mexico: The Tiangui handout
paper and pencils
colored pencils, markers, paints
scissors
optional: objects created in other activities (e.g., tin ornaments, nearikas) to "sell" in the marketplace
video or photographs showing Mexican marketplace
photographs or examples of Mexican currency

BACKGROUND

In Mexico, there are many different ways of shopping. In metropolitan areas, supermarkets and department stores are just like their counterparts in other parts of the world. They offer a broad range of goods, with clearly marked prices. But the *tiangui*—the traditional market—is another way to shop. In the tiangui, handmade items are found side by side with plastic toys and radios. The market is a social and business event, where both local gossip and goods exchange hands in a friendly, bargaining atmosphere. Here, the prices of items are not clearly marked; except for a few items (like food, drink, and candies), prices are usually open to negotiation.

PROCEDURE

1. Brainstorm with the class the kinds of markets they have seen. Ideas might include flea markets, farmers' markets, supermarkets, garage sales. Next, ask what kind of things they think might be found in a Mexican market. Ideas might include clothes, food, and handmade items. Next, have students make predictions about the appearance and atmosphere of a Mexican market. What might it look like? Sound like? Smell like? If possible, show a video or photographs of a Mexican market.

2. If you can, show students photographs or examples of Mexican currency. Direct students to prepare "currency" in the denominations specified on the handout: two notes each of 100, 500, 1000, 2000, 5000, and 10,000 pesos; and ten "coins" each of 1, 5, 10, and 50 pesos and of 20 and 50 centavos.
3. If actual craft items are available, distribute them to students. Students decide on the price (in pesos) of each item. If actual items are not available, students should prepare paper representations of goods for sale.
4. Discuss the concept of bargaining. If you like, give students vocabulary words and phrases for shopping in Spanish.
5. Model selling an item to a student. You should act the role of vendor. First, have the student greet the vendor. Then quote a price for the item. Next, encourage the student to offer a lower price. Repeat two or three times until a compromise is reached.
6. Divide class into pairs. Now have the students practice in twos, taking turns as both buyer and seller.
7. Set up the market stalls with items for sale. Set a time limit for the first transaction. Open the market. When the first transaction has been completed, students switch roles and complete a second transaction.

Extension Activities

- Have students create a background mural for their market.
- Have students determine the Spanish for the words and phrases they will need to use in bargaining, including the words for numbers. Students first practice using the Spanish words, and then conduct the activity in Spanish.
- When all transactions have been completed, divide the class into small groups. Each group member should state one thing he or she liked and one thing he or she didn't like about the bargaining process.

Name ______________________________ Date ______________

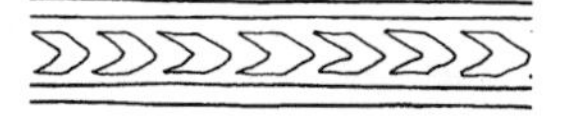

Shopping in Mexico: The Tiangui

For centuries, the Mexican marketplace—the ***tiangui***—has been a striking sight. The first Spaniards to arrive in Mexico in 1521 were amazed by the markets they saw. One soldier, Bernal Diaz di Castillo, wrote this description of the marketplace:

> We turned to look at the great marketplace and the crowds of people that were in it, some buying and others selling, so that the murmur and hum of their voices could be heard more than a league off. Some of the soldiers among us who had been in many parts of the world, in Constantinople, and all over Italy, and in Rome, said that so large a marketplace and so well and regularly attended, they had never beheld before.

Today in most parts of Mexico, you can buy anything you like in fine shops and department stores. But the traditional market, either outdoors or in a market hall, still exists. In rural areas, the outdoor market is important for both social and economic reasons. Friends meet there to exchange news. Weavers, potters, and other artisans sell their goods there and then buy the things they need themselves. Market day is that time when locals hawk their wares, entertain tourists, and discuss the week's events. Parents, children, and grandparents often attend together.

Market day is very long for the sellers. They often have to travel long distances from their villages. Usually, the first arrivals get the best positions to display their wares on tables, in the back of trucks, or even on the ground. Sometimes the fresh produce is all together, and the jewelry and the other crafts are arranged in logical groupings. Markets open early, so buyers who want the best selections also arrive very early in the morning.

The entire market area is filled with stalls. You can buy hand-coiled pots, woven shoulder bags, wooden baskets, lacquered gourds. There are stalls filled with toys and stalls piled high with fresh fruit. The prices on things are not fixed; everyone haggles to set a final price. The seller names a price. The buyer suggests a lower price. They bargain back and forth—the seller lowering the asking price, the buyer increasing the price offered—until they reach a price they both agree on. Then the money and the item change hands, and the deal is concluded. The whole exchange might go something like this:

Pottery bowls lined up at a Mexican marketplace

(continued)

Name ______________________________ Date ______________

Shopping in Mexico: The Tiangui *(continued)*

Buyer: Good morning.

Seller: Yes, it's a beautiful morning, isn't it?

Buyer: Well, it looks as if it might rain. In fact, I've been thinking of buying an umbrella. How much are the ones here?

Seller: Ah, these are excellent umbrellas, at a very good price. I am asking only 150 pesos for these umbrellas.

Buyer: 150 pesos! Oh, no, that would be too much for me. I will offer you 75 pesos for an umbrella.

Seller: I'm afraid I could not accept 75 pesos for one of these fine umbrellas. What about 120 pesos?

Buyer: 85 pesos.

Seller: 110 pesos.

Buyer: 95 pesos.

Seller: 100 pesos.

Buyer: All right, 100 pesos it is. Here you go. And thank you very much!

Try setting up your own tiangui and bargaining for goods.

1. First, you will need to have some money. The currency in Mexico is the **peso**. The peso is divided into 100 **centavos**. Bank notes come in denominations of 100, 500, 1000, 2000, 5000, and 10,000 pesos. Make two bank notes of each of these denominations. There are coins of 1, 5, 10, and 50 pesos, as well as coins of 20 and 50 centavos. Make ten "coins" of each of these denominations.

2. You will need to have something to sell at the tiangui. If you do not have any Mexican objects to offer, make a drawing of something that might be found in a Mexican market. This will be the item that you are selling. What is the value of your item? Decide on the price—in pesos—you would like to sell it for. Then decide on a higher price to give as your asking price. Remember, the "buyer" will expect to bargain. If you start by asking the "real" price, you'll end up getting a lot less than you wanted.

A 2,000-peso note

3. Follow your teacher's directions to "buy" and "sell" at the market.

Connect-the-Dots Geography

Teacher Guide Page

Objectives

Social Studies

- Students will use grid coordinates to find geographic locations.
- Students will use coordinates to map a region.
- Students will try to identify the region they map.
- Students will learn the approximate latitude and longitude of one or more countries in Central America.

Math

- Students will practice using grid coordinates to map points.

Art

- Students will use grid coordinates to create a "connect-the-dots" map of Central America.

Materials

Connect-the-Dots Geography handout
optional: map of Central America

Prerequisites

Students should know how to find grid coordinates and map points on a grid.

Preparation

1. To make each grid easier to work on, you may want to enlarge the grids on a copier. Be sure to enlarge all the grids by the same amount, so that the scale on all finished maps will be the same.
2. With some students, you may want to give a little extra support by mapping, numbering, and connecting a few points (or groups of points) before copying the grid. That way students will know if they're on the right track as they go along.

Procedure

1. This works well as a group activity, with one group mapping each country, or with all groups mapping the same country at one time. Since several countries call for locating and connecting dozens of points, you may want to assign the first half of the numbers to one group and the second half to another group, or assign different groups to different countries.
2. Divide the class into groups. Distribute the reproducible pages to the groups. Ask students to guess what the pairs of numbers are, and how they might relate to the country named at the top of each reproducible. Students should

recognize that the pairs of numbers give the latitude and longitude of geographic locations in each country.

3. If you want, make a transparency of one of the grids and model the procedure on the overhead projector. Students should start with the first pair of coordinates, find that location on the grid, and make a dot at that point. Number the point "1." The next point should be numbered "2," and so forth, until all the coordinates have been located, mapped, and numbered. The first and last coordinates map the same point. Students should write both numbers by the point. Point out that the grid includes only whole numbers, but many of the coordinates include decimal points. How can students decide where to locate these coordinates? How would the map change if you ignored the decimals and used only the whole numbers for the coordinates?
4. When all the coordinates have been mapped, students should start at the point numbered "1" and connect the dots. If they have located the coordinates correctly, they should have a rough map of the country named at the top of the handout. Students can compare their maps with an atlas to see how each map resembles the actual country, and how it is different. (Students have mapped 20–30 points along the country's perimeter, so a great deal of the detail is lost. To make mapping easier, we have used approximate coordinates, not precise ones.)
5. Since all the maps use the same grid, all the maps are to the same approximate scale. If you want, ask students to determine what the scale is. (Scale depends on whether you enlarged the grids before distributing them.) Have them add the scale to their maps.
6. What different uses do we have for maps? Ask students how useful a map like this would be, and to whom.

Extension Activities

- The coordinates given on the handout describe the perimeter of each country. Have students name the capital of the country they have mapped. They should then find the city's latitude and longitude and locate the city on the map, using a star instead of a point. They can add the capital's coordinates to the list of coordinates on the handout.
- Photocopy all the maps, and give each group a copy of each map. Students should cut along the outline of each map, then tape them together to create an overall map of the region.
- Have students create a large version of the grid, using the same scale. They can use the coordinates on the next page to create a similar map of Mexico.

Grid Coordinates: Mexico

1. 26 97.5
2. 22.5 98
3. 20 96.5
4. 18 94.5
5. 18.5 91.5
6. 20 90.75
7. 21 90.7
8. 21.5 87
9. 20 87.5
10. 18 88
11. 18.5 88.5
12. 18 89
13. 17.8 91
14. 17.25 91
15. 17.25 91.4
16. 16.4 90.4
17. 16.1 90.4
18. 16.1 91.75
19. 15.25 92.25
20. 14.5 92.25
21. 16.25 95
22. 15.75 96.5
23. 17 100
24. 18.5 103.5
25. 20.4 105.7
26. 21.5 105
27. 24 107
28. 25.5 109.5
29. 32 115
30. 30 114.5
31. 28 113
32. 23.25 109.5
33. 23 110
34. 28 115
35. 28 114
36. 29.5 115.75
37. 32.5 115
38. 32.8 115
39. 31.3 111
40. 31.3 108.2
41. 31.8 108.2
42. 31.8 106.2
43. 29.4 104.4
44. 29 103.2
45. 29.8 102.7
46. 29.8 101.7
47. 26.2 99
48. 26 97.5

Name ______________________________ Date ______________

Connect-the-Dots Geography: Belize

Follow your teacher's directions to find these points on the grid below. Then connect the dots in order from 1 to 18.

1. 18.5 N 88.5 W
2. 18.4 N 88.25 W
3. 18.3 N 88 W
4. 18.1 N 88 W
5. 18 N 88.1 W
6. 17.6 N 88.3 W
7. 17.5 N 88.2 W
8. 17 N 88.25 W
9. 16.5 N 88.4 W
10. 16.25 N 88.6 W
11. 16.1 N 88.8 W
12. 15.8 N 88.9 W
13. 15.9 N 89.3 W
14. 17.8 N 89.2 W
15. 17.9 N 89.2 W
16. 18 N 89 W
17. 17.9 N 88.8 W
18. 18.5 N 88.5 W

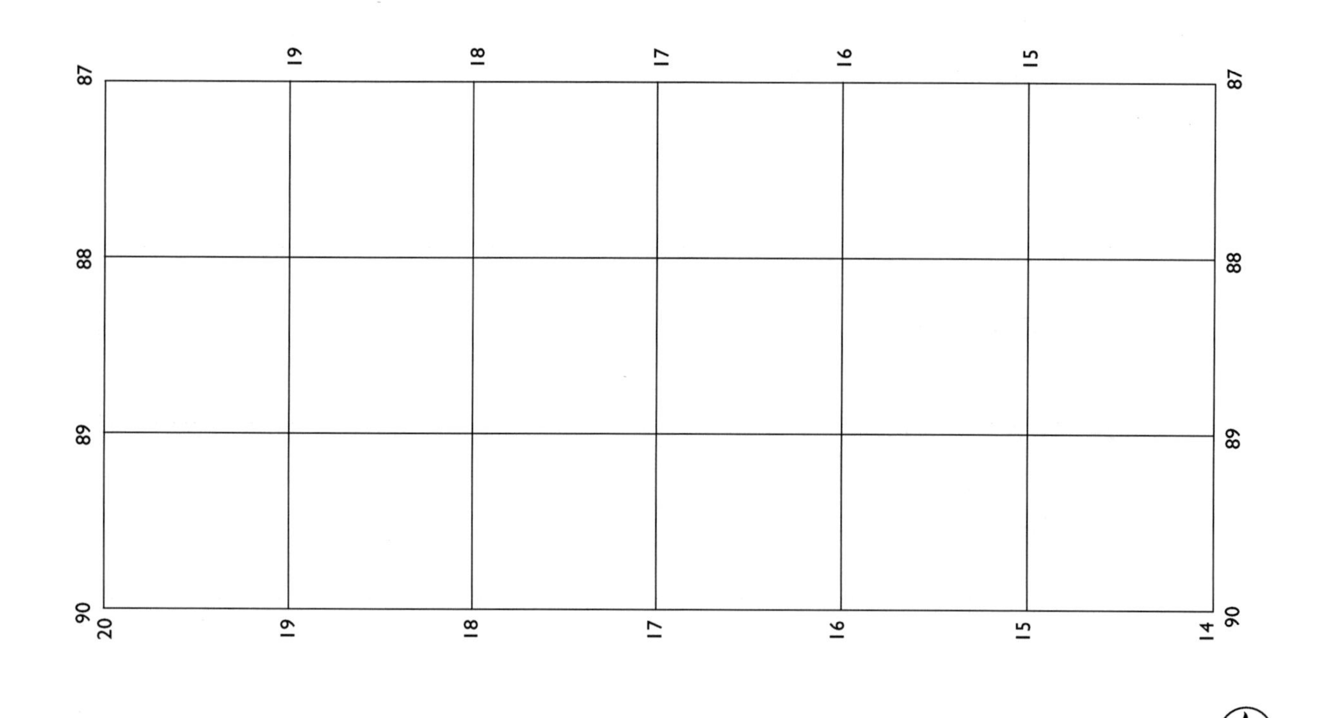

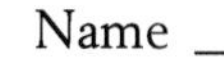

Name ______________________ Date ______________

Connect-the-Dots Geography: Costa Rica

Follow your teacher's directions to find these points on the grid below. Then connect the dots in order from 1 to 30.

1.	11 N	85.7 W	11.	9.5 N	84.5 W	21.	9.7 N	82.8 W
2.	10.9 N	85.7 W	12.	9 N	83.6 W	22.	9.6 N	82.6 W
3.	10.9 N	85.9 W	13.	8.6 N	83.8 W	23.	10 N	83 W
4.	10.8 N	85.7 W	14.	8 N	82.9 W	24.	10.5 N	83.5 W
5.	10.5 N	85.8 W	15.	8.4 N	83.1 W	25.	10.9 N	83.7 W
6.	10 N	85.7 W	16.	8.5 N	82.8 W	26.	10.8 N	83.9 W
7.	9.8 N	85.2 W	17.	8.8 N	82.9 W	27.	11.1 N	84.7 W
8.	9.5 N	85.1 W	18.	8.9 N	82.7 W	28.	10.9 N	84.9 W
9.	10 N	84.7 W	19.	9.1 N	82.9 W	29.	11.2 N	85.6 W
10.	9.7 N	84.6 W	20.	9.5 N	82.9 W	30.	11 N	85.8 W

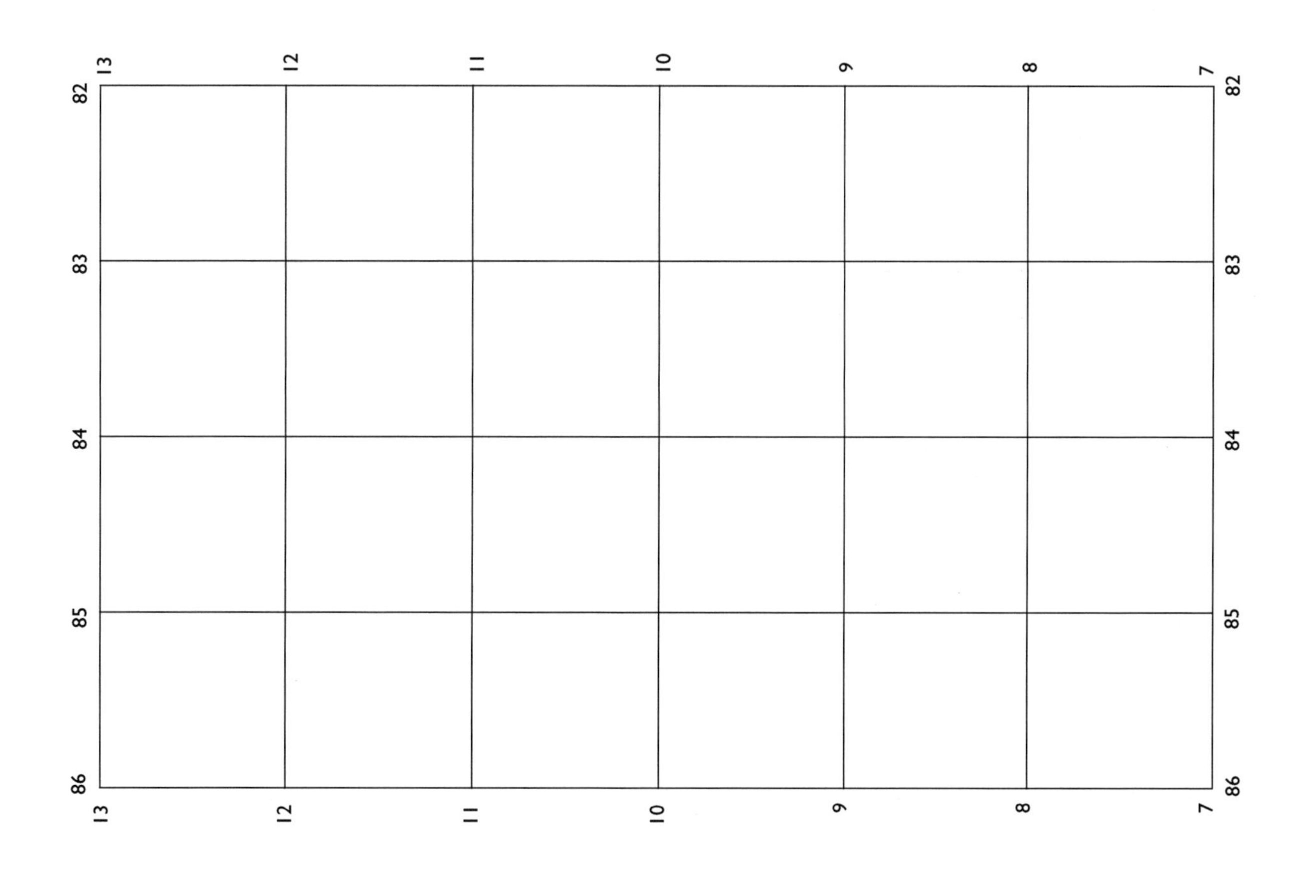

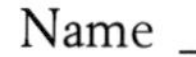

Name ______________________________ Date ________________

Connect-the-Dots Geography: El Salvador

Follow your teacher's directions to find these points on the grid below. Then connect the dots in order from 1 to 17.

1. 13.75 N 90.1 W
2. 14 N 90 W
3. 14 N 89.75 W
4. 14.2 N 89.7 W
5. 14.25 N 89.5 W
6. 14.4 N 89.6 W
7. 14.4 N 89.4 W
8. 13.8 N 88.5 W
9. 13.9 N 88.25 W
10. 13.8 N 87.6 W
11. 13.4 N 87.8 W
12. 13.2 N 87.9 W
13. 13.2 N 88.5 W
14. 13.5 N 89.3 W
15. 13.6 N 89.75 W
16. 13.7 N 89.8 W
17. 13.75 N 90.1 W

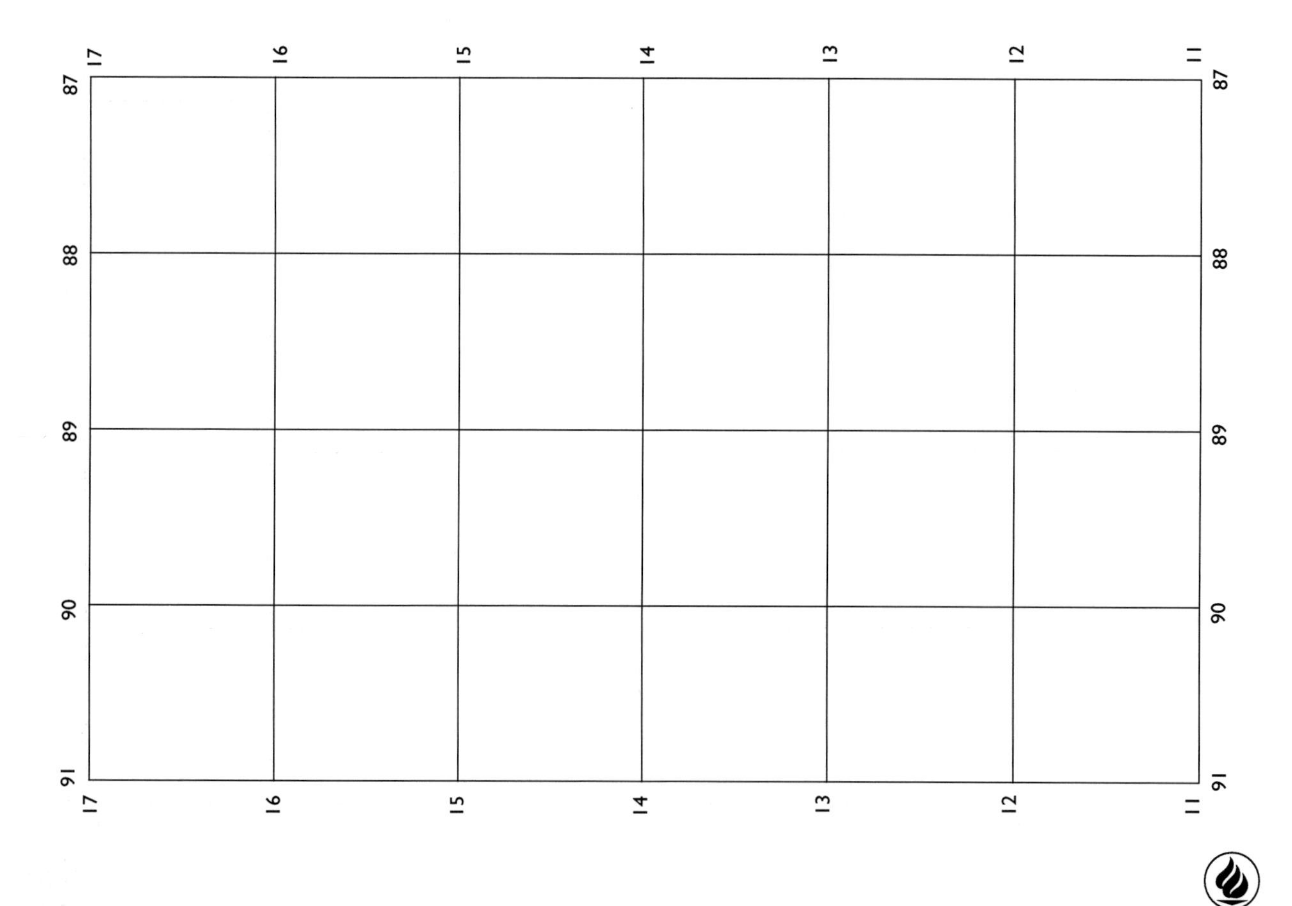

Name ______________________________ Date ______________

Connect-the-Dots Geography: Guatemala

Follow your teacher's directions to find these points on the grid below. Then connect the dots in order from 1 to 25.

1. 14.5 N 92.25 W
2. 15 N 92.1 W
3. 15.25 N 92.25 W
4. 16.1 N 91.75 W
5. 16.1 N 90.4 W
6. 16.4 N 90.4 W
7. 17.25 N 91.45 W
8. 17.25 N 91 W
9. 17.8 N 91 W
10. 17.8 N 89.2 W
11. 15.9 N 89.3 W
12. 15.8 N 88.9 W
13. 15.75 N 88.25 W
14. 15.1 N 89.2 W
15. 14.6 N 89.2 W
16. 14.4 N 89.4 W
17. 14.4 N 89.6 W
18. 14.25 N 89.5 W
19. 14.2 N 89.7 W
20. 14 N 89.75 W
21. 14 N 90 W
22. 13.75 N 90.1 W
23. 13.9 N 90.8 W
24. 14.1 N 91.5 W
25. 14.5 N 92.25 W

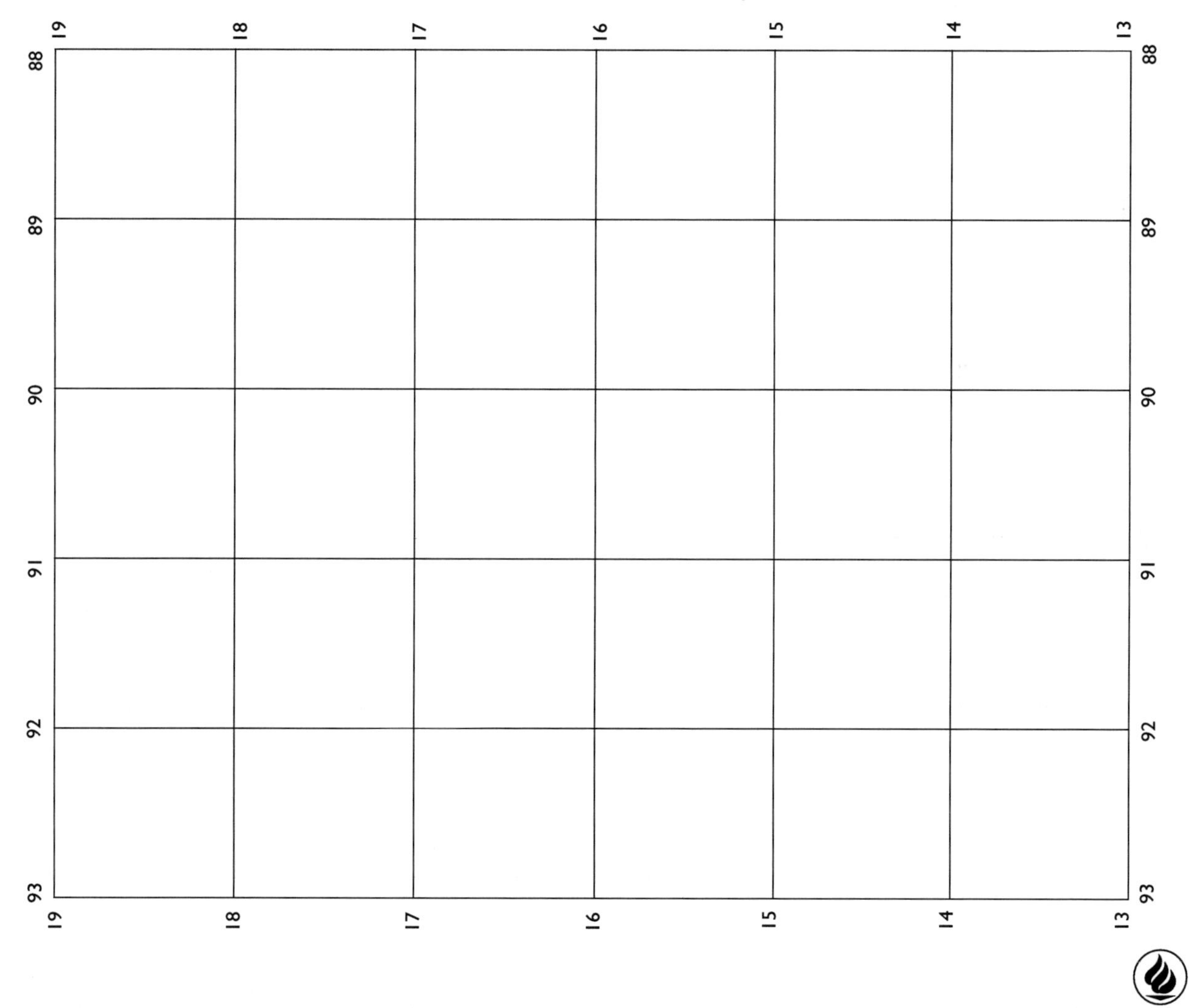

Name ______________________________ Date ______________

Connect-the-Dots Geography: Honduras

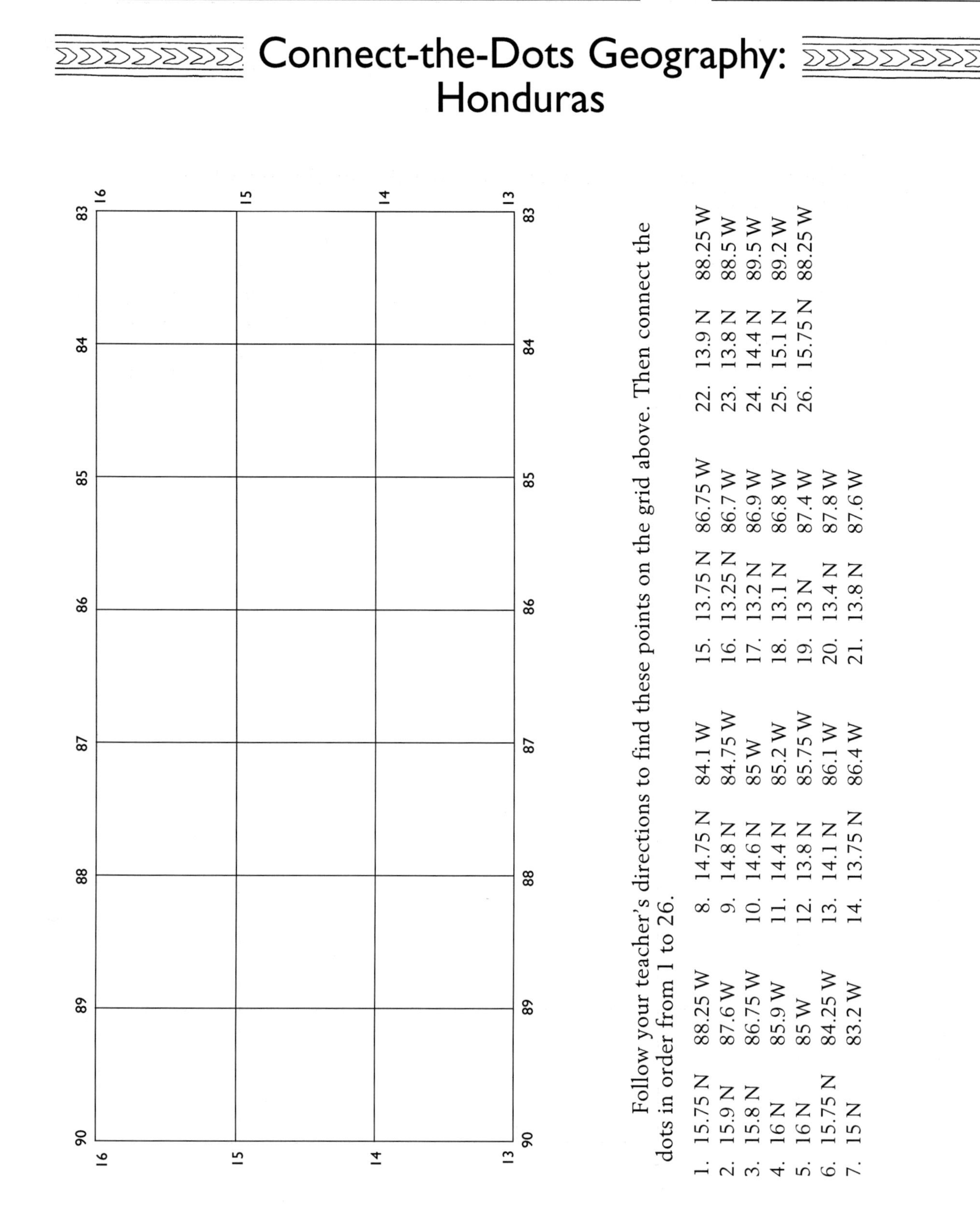

Follow your teacher's directions to find these points on the grid above. Then connect the dots in order from 1 to 26.

1. 15.75 N 88.25 W
2. 15.9 N 87.6 W
3. 15.8 N 86.75 W
4. 16 N 85.9 W
5. 16 N 85 W
6. 15.75 N 84.25 W
7. 15 N 83.2 W
8. 14.75 N 84.1 W
9. 14.8 N 84.75 W
10. 14.6 N 85 W
11. 14.4 N 85.2 W
12. 13.8 N 85.75 W
13. 14.1 N 86.1 W
14. 13.75 N 86.4 W
15. 13.75 N 86.75 W
16. 13.25 N 86.7 W
17. 13.2 N 86.9 W
18. 13.1 N 86.8 W
19. 13 N 87.4 W
20. 13.4 N 87.8 W
21. 13.8 N 87.6 W
22. 13.9 N 88.25 W
23. 13.8 N 88.5 W
24. 14.4 N 89.5 W
25. 15.1 N 89.2 W
26. 15.75 N 88.25 W

Name ______________________________ Date ______________

Connect-the-Dots Geography: Nicaragua

Follow your teacher's directions to find these points on the grid below. Then connect the dots in order from 1 to 27.

1.	13 N	87.4 W	8.	13.8 N	85.75 W	15.	12.9 N	83.5 W	22.	10.9 N	84.8 W
2.	13.1 N	86.8 W	9.	14.4 N	85.2 W	16.	11.6 N	83.6 W	23.	11.2 N	85.6 W
3.	13.2 N	86.9 W	10.	14.6 N	85 W	17.	11.25 N	83.8 W	24.	11 N	85.75 W
4.	13.25 N	86.7 W	11.	14.8 N	84.75 W	18.	11 N	83.75 W	25.	11.5 N	86.1 W
5.	13.75 N	86.75 W	12.	14.75 N	84.1 W	19.	10.9 N	83.6 W	26.	12.8 N	87.75 W
6.	13.75 N	86.4 W	13.	15 N	83.2 W	20.	10.75 N	83.9 W	27.	13 N	87.4 W
7.	14.1 N	86.1 W	14.	14.25 N	83.25 W	21.	11.1 N	84.6 W			

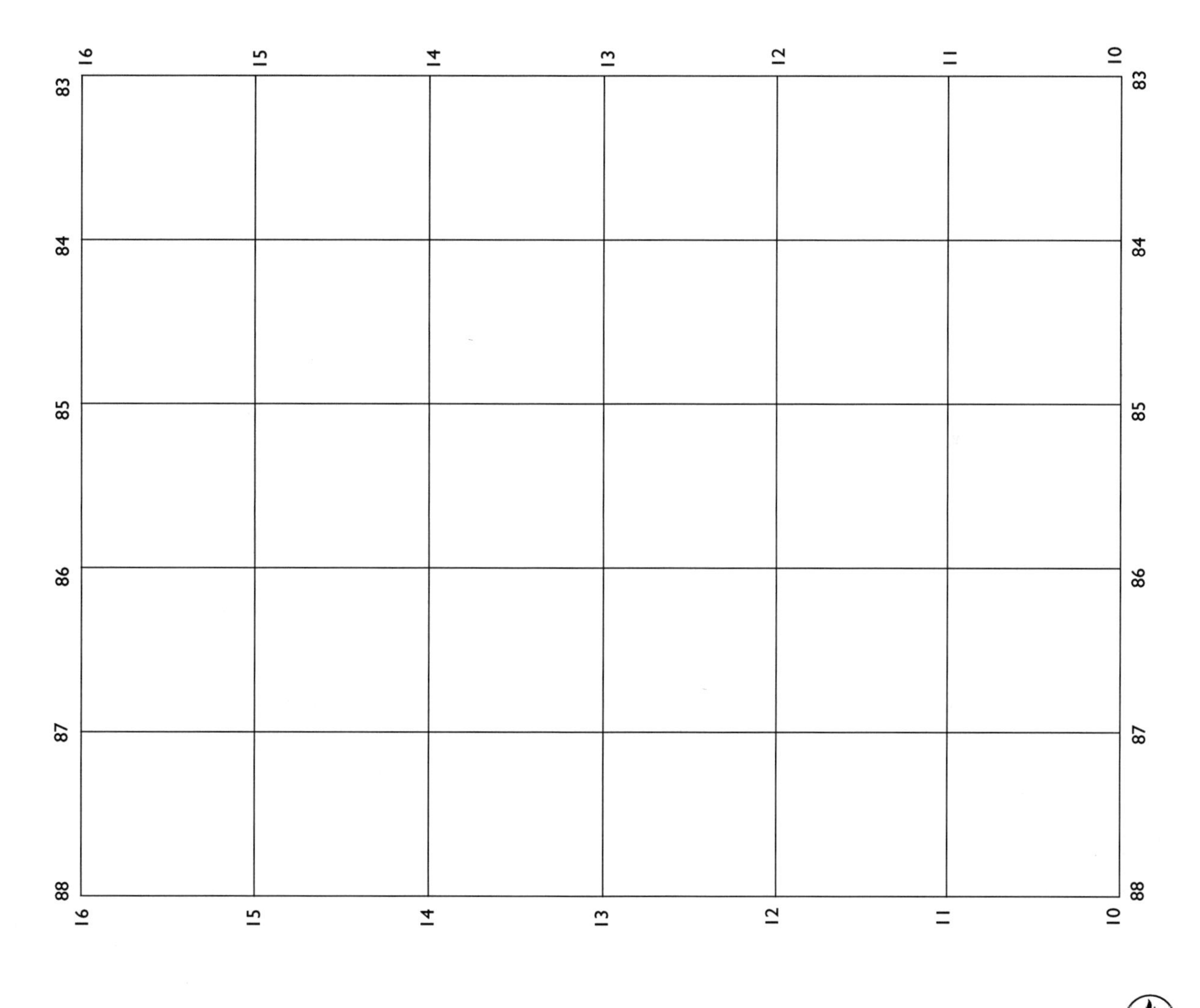

Name ______________________________ Date ______________

Connect-the-Dots Geography: Panama

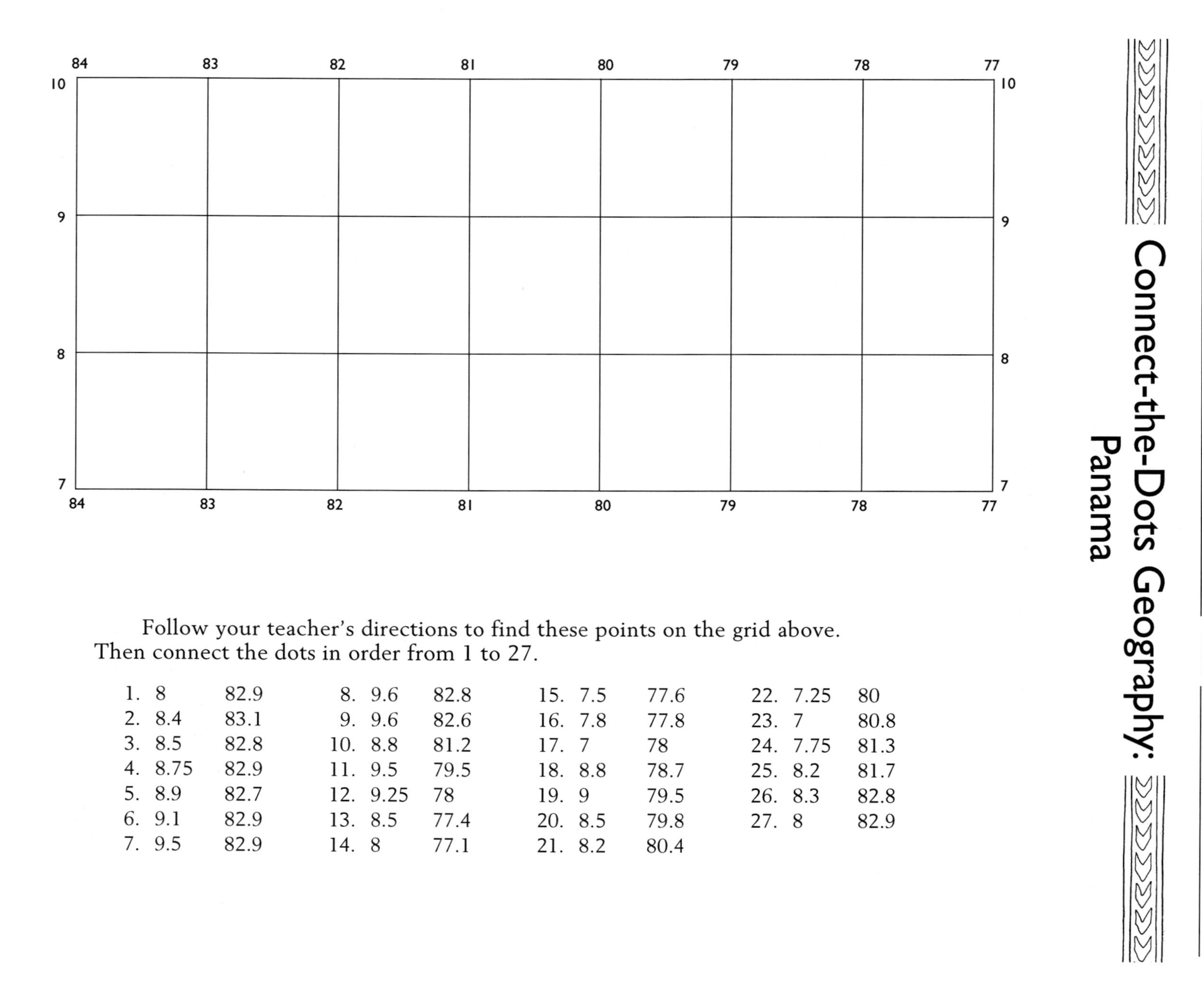

Follow your teacher's directions to find these points on the grid above.
Then connect the dots in order from 1 to 27.

1.	8	82.9	8.	9.6	82.8	15.	7.5	77.6	22.	7.25	80
2.	8.4	83.1	9.	9.6	82.6	16.	7.8	77.8	23.	7	80.8
3.	8.5	82.8	10.	8.8	81.2	17.	7	78	24.	7.75	81.3
4.	8.75	82.9	11.	9.5	79.5	18.	8.8	78.7	25.	8.2	81.7
5.	8.9	82.7	12.	9.25	78	19.	9	79.5	26.	8.3	82.8
6.	9.1	82.9	13.	8.5	77.4	20.	8.5	79.8	27.	8	82.9
7.	9.5	82.9	14.	8	77.1	21.	8.2	80.4			

Resources

General

Bartok, Mira. *Ancient Mexico.* Glenview, IL: Scott-Foresman, 1993. This book includes six stencils that students could use for craft projects, a map of ancient cultures, descriptions of rituals and games, and myths. It is an excellent resource for students to use with very little supervision.

Culturegrams. Provo, Utah: Brigham Young University, Center for International and Area Studies, 1992. Tel: (800) 528-6279. This is a series of four-page leaflets about the countries of the world. It is native commentary and original, expert analysis but very clear and easy for students to use. Each report contains greetings, visiting, eating, and gestures. It also gives an overview of the people, lifestyle, nation, and traveler's advice.

Cultures of the World (series). Tarrytown, NY: Marshall Cavendish.

Enchantment of the World (series). Chicago: Children's Press.

Enciso, George. *Designs from Pre-Columbian Mexico.* New York: Dover Publications, Inc., 1971.

Gibbs, Virginia G. L*atin America Curriculum Materials for the Middle Grades.* Milwaukee: University of Wisconsin, Center for Latin America, 1985. This source has two excellent activities. One is a classroom marketplace to simulate the Aztec version and the other is an economics activity to identify the origins of products made outside the U.S.

Lirse, Barbara, and Dick Judd. *Fiesta: Mexico and Central America.* Fearon Teacher Aids. Paramount Communications Co., 1993. This is a music, craft, and recipe resource for fiestas.

Nelson, Catherine E., and Betty N. West. *A Survey of World Cultures: Latin America.* American Guidance Service, 1990. A complete guide to the culture and history of Latin America.

Pettit, Florence H. and Robert M. *Mexican Folk Toys.* New York: Hastings House, 1978. This is a beautifully illustrated book of folk toys arranged by seasonal celebrations.

http://lanic.utexas.edu/la/region.html
This is the University of Texas Latin American Studies main site. It is loaded with up-to-date information like maps, weather, and hurricane updates.

http://www.folkart.com/~latitude/home/mex.htm
This is a sampling of Mexican folk art and crafts.

http://libwww.essex.ac.uk/./news.html
This is a collection of newspapers: five Mexican and one Costa Rican.

Money and Trade

http://www.xe.net/currency/
This site converts from various currencies, including $US, to other currencies.

http://www.xe.net.cgi-bin/curtable
A currency table is created showing major currencies in the base currency of your choice.

http://pacific.commerce.ubc.ca/xr/yplot.html
This site will assemble a diagram comparing up to five different currencies of your choice.

Folktales

Lyons, Grant, ed. *Tales the People Tell in Mexico.* New York: Simon and Schuster, Inc., 1992. A series of tales from Mexico with a glossary of Spanish words and their meanings.

The Maya Codex

The Nuttall Codex. New York: Dover Books.

Several Web sites offer information about, and images from, Aztec codices, which are similar in many ways to Maya codices.

http://www.Realtime.net/maya/aztecfldr/Rios.html
This site gives short explanations about different parts of the Codex Rios.

http://pages.prodigy.com/GBonline/awaztec.html
Some of the text on this site is challenging, but it provides great images from a variety of codices.

http://www.mexico-virtual.com/~nagual.codex
Some of the vocabulary used here is difficult, but it gives detailed information about the glyphs of the Codex Mendoza.

Cooking in Mexico

Coronado, Rosa. *Cooking the Mexican Way.* Minneapolis: Lerner Publications, 1982.

http://soar.berkeley.edu/recipes/ethnic/mexican/indexall.html
This site provides recipes for a number of Mexican dishes; it also has recipes from other ethnic cuisines.

A Conversation in . . .

http://www.sil.org/lla
This site offers detailed information about the hundreds of languages spoken in Mexico and Central America today. Information includes the language name, language family, number of speakers, and region in which it is spoken.

A Conversation in Mayan

http://indy4.fdl.cc.mu.us/~isk/maya/mayatab1.html
This site gives information about the Maya language.

A Conversation in Spanish

http://www.travlang.com/languages
This site offers simple phrases translated from English into a number of different languages, including Spanish. Sound files with pronunciations are also included. The files are large, so access can be slow. An online "quiz" for each language is also offered.

Panama: Molas

Caraway, Caren. *The Mola Design Book.* Owings Mills, Maryland: Stemmer House, 1981.

Nearika: Yarn Paintings

The Fine Arts Museum of San Francisco. *Art of the Huichol Indians.* New York: Harry N. Abrams, Inc., 1980.

Shopping in Mexico: The Tiangui

Latin American Curriculum Resource Center. Center for Latin American Studies. 105 Hebert Building, Tulane University, New Orleans, LA 70118-5698. Tel: (504) 865-5164 Fax: (504) 865-6719. This center has five slide sets of markets in Ecuador, Guatemala, Peru, Mexico, and Latin America. Each set has 10 slides and a guide.

http://homepage.interaccess.com/~mar/openair.html
Openair-Market Net: The World Wide Guide to Farmers' Markets, Street Markets, Flea Markets, and Street Vendors.

Glossary

appliqué	fabric-decorating technique in which shaped sections of cloth are sewn to a fabric background
Aztec	early civilization in Mexico
balboa	currency of Panama
Belize dollar	currency of Belize
calaveras	skeleton figures; part of Mexico's Day of the Dead celebration
codex	folded paper book
colon	currency of El Salvador
conquistador	Spanish word meaning "conqueror," term applied to the Spanish invaders led by Hernan Cortés
cordoba	currency of Nicaragua
Costa Rican colon	currency of Costa Rica
Cuna Indians	people who live on Panama's San Blas Islands
Día de los Muertos	Day of the Dead, celebrated in Mexico from November 1 to November 2
fiesta	festival, party
Huichol Indians	people who live in Mexico's Sierra Madre
lempira	currency of Honduras
matracas	rattle, often made in the shape of an animal or bird
Maya	early civilization in Mexico and Central America
Mexican peso	currency of Mexico
molas	reverse appliqué panels created by the Cuna Indians of Panama
mole, mole poblano	Mexican sauce, often used for chicken, which contains a number of different ingredients, including unsweetened chocolate
mural	wall painting
nearika	paintings in yarn created by the Huichol Indians of Mexico
ofrenda	table of offerings prepared as part of the Day of the Dead festivities

papier-mâché	material consisting of paper pulp or layers of paper attached with paste
quetzal	currency of Guatemala, named for a tropical bird
reverse appliqué	fabric-decorating technique in which sections of fabric are cut away to reveal other layers of fabric below
tiangui	traditional Mexican open-air market

We want to hear from you! Your valuable comments and suggestions will help us meet your current and future classroom needs.

Your name____________________ Date__________

School name____________________ Phone__________

School address____________________

Grade level taught______ Subject area(s) taught__________ Average class size_____

Where did you purchase this publication?____________________

Was your salesperson knowledgeable about this product? Yes____ No____

What monies were used to purchase this product?

___School supplemental budget ___Federal/state funding ___Personal

Please "grade" this Walch publication according to the following criteria:

Quality of service you received when purchasing	A	B	C	D	F
Ease of use	A	B	C	D	F
Quality of content	A	B	C	D	F
Page layout	A	B	C	D	F
Organization of material	A	B	C	D	F
Suitability for grade level	A	B	C	D	F
Instructional value	A	B	C	D	F

COMMENTS:____________________

What specific supplemental materials would help you meet your current—or future—instructional needs?

Have you used other Walch publications? If so, which ones?____________________

May we use your comments in upcoming communications? ___Yes ___No

Please **FAX** this completed form to **207-772-3105**, or mail it to:

Product Development, J.Weston Walch, Publisher, P.O. Box 658, Portland, ME 04104-0658

We will send you a **FREE GIFT** as our way of thanking you for your feedback. **THANK YOU!**